Psycholinguistics
DEVELOPMENTAL AND PATHOLOGICAL

Psycholinguistics

DEVELOPMENTAL AND PATHOLOGICAL

Edited by John Morton and John C. Marshall

EVE V. CLARK
DAVID BLOOR
JOANNA RYAN
JOHN C. MARSHALL

Cornell University Press
Ithaca, New York

First published 1977 by Cornell University Press

International Standard Book Number 0-8014-1075-4
Library of Congress Catalog Card Number 76-28019

Printed in Great Britain by
Unwin Brothers Limited,
The Gresham Press, Old Woking, Surrey

Contents

Preface

This is the first in a group of volumes intended to meet what is to us a major need. Most books on psycholinguistics, we find, are restricted in scope, even if they manage to cover one area in reasonable depth. Journal articles, on the other hand, are seldom of sufficient length to be of other than local use. It is not even always clear what might reasonably be considered to be the facts. Experiments which on first sight seem to represent major advances soon turn out to be full of methodological or conceptual flaws. The refutations in the literature are easily missed, and the myths remain.

Furthermore, the subjects of related interest to psycholinguistics —linguistics, neurology, computer science—are so diverse in the conventional classification that one cannot hope to remain both informed and sane.

What we plan to do, then, is to provide constructive surveys of the state of particular aspects of psycholinguistics and these related subjects, and to give detailed and critical accounts of important growth areas. Incidentally, our use of 'psycholinguistics' should not be taken to imply a particular restriction of topic or outlook. For us the term is broader in size and shorter in length than 'the psychology of language' and more specific than 'cognition' or 'communication studies'. We hope that our use of the term will help to broaden its definition.

The next volumes will include sections on second language learning, applying the psychology of language, word recognition, prose recall, speech perception in infants, and an outline of the current state of linguistic thought. Further planned contributions include human speech perception, word recognition, computer recognition of speech, sign language. We do *not* invite manuscripts, but we do invite suggestions for suitable topics or possible writers.

John Morton (MRC Applied
Psychology Unit, Cambridge)
John C. Marshall (Interfakultaire
Werkgroep Taal-en
Spraakgedrag,
University of Nijmegen)

vii

First Language Acquisition

EVE V. CLARK
Assistant Professor, Department of Linguistics,
Stanford University

2

CONTENTS

The impetus for research on first language acquisition in the last two decades has come largely from linguistic theory. Chomsky (e.g., 1957, 1959, 1965, 1968), in particular, was extremely influential in re-opening a field of enquiry that had long been of interest to psychologists and linguists alike (Blumenthal, 1970). The questions posed as a result of the theoretical assumptions about the acquisition of language led to much more rigorous observation of the structures used by children. The emphasis on sentential structure and the expression of structural relations was undoubtedly a reflection of the emphasis on syntax and syntactic structure within transformational generative linguistic theory. More recently, however, both in linguistics and in the study of first language acquisition by children, there has been a shift in emphasis to considering not only syntax but also semantics, cognition, and the communicative functions of language. This broader perspective is the natural outcome of applying more rigorous analysis to the child language data: too many questions remained unanswered, and unanswerable, within the narrower framework of syntax alone.

The present review of some of the more recent research in first language acquisition will concentrate on some of the insights gained by taking into account certain semantic factors in the analysis of child language. In most areas, adequate theories of language acquisition still remain to be formulated. The reader who seeks an integrated view of all aspects of language acquisition may therefore be disappointed by the present state of the art. However, the growing interest in finding out about language acquisition in a broad perspective can only be encouraging to the researcher in the field.

The present chapter has been organized under five main headings: sentence structure, semantic development, language and cognitive development, child phonology, and language input to young children. Within each section, I shall discuss some of the recent trends in research, and attempt to place them in a general framework in which language is regarded as a system of communication, used to convey both fact and emotion, and bound therefore both by cognitive constraints and by social factors. In general, I shall concentrate on research carried out in the last five years or so between 1968 and 1973). Earlier work has been ably reviewed in a number of places (e.g., Braine, 1971; McCarthy, 1954) to which the reader will be referred when necessary and for a more recent overview, the reader can consult Clark and Clark (1977).[1]

SENTENCE STRUCTURE

In this section, I will first consider the importance of proposing a general theory of speech acts for dealing with the acquisition of language. From this viewpoint, one can retain hold of the fact that language is a social tool for communication in treating it as a system with a complex syntactic, semantic and phonological structure. My second topic follows from the first: the analysis of grammatical relations (e.g., subject-of, verb-of) in the young child's speech. Since most investigators have considered that the child's syntax only becomes accessible when he begins to combine two or more words, the one-word stage has generally been ignored. However, a theory that included an account of the functions of different utterances might provide some insights for the one-word stage as well.

Once the child has begun to use two-word utterances, he begins to acquire the inflexions that mark certain grammatical relations, e.g., the possessive 's in English. The acquisition of such inflexions forms the third topic of this section. Lastly, I shall discuss some studies of more complex sentence structures in children's speech, including various types of subordinate clauses and complements.

Utterance functions

A potential truism in the study of language is that when the speaker says something, he is assumed to have some intention behind his utterance. At the most general level, this intention is to affect the addressee in some predictable way, such that the addressee supplies the speaker with needed information (as in answering a question), confirms some hypothesis, responds to a request, and so on. These communicative functions of language have attracted the attention of both philosophers and linguists who have analysed different *speech acts* and made preliminary attempts to describe the conditions pertaining to their use in terms of *conversational postulates* (e.g., Austin, 1962; Searle, 1970, 1971; Grice, 1967; Ross, 1970; Gordon

1. The preparation of this chapter in 1973, and the author's research reported therein, was supported in part by the National Science Foundation, Grant No. GS-30040. I would like to thank Herbert H. Clark, Susan E. Haviland and John Morton for their helpful comments and suggestions on an earlier version.

and Lakoff, 1970). Austin (1962), for example, distinguished between 'performative' and 'constative' utterances, the difference being that the former allow no separation of the utterance from the act described in it, e.g., *I (hereby) christen this ship the Usquebaugh* or *I promise to eat the eel*. In an extension of some of Austin's proposals, Ross (1970) argued that all speech acts are preceded by a performative, but in many instances this performative is of a very abstract nature and has no realization in the surface form of the utterance. For example, Ross suggested that all assertions contain the underlying performative '[I assert to you that] Sentence', imperatives contain something like '[I order you] Sentence', and questions something like '[I request you-you tell me] Sentence'. In addition, one needs to account for the fact that a single sentence form may have a number of functions, and a single communicative function may be expressed using a number of different sentence forms. For example, the speaker may convey a request to his addressee to open the window in any of the following ways: directly, with *Open the window*, or slightly more politely with *Please open the window*; more politely still, *Would you open the window, please?*, and less directly, *Could you open the window, please?*. Or, the speaker may say *The window needs opening, The window's shut, is it?*, and even *It's hot in here*, to achieve the same effect (e.g., Gordon and Lakoff, 1970). At the same time, one *normally* uses affirmative statements to make assertions, interrogatives to ask questions, imperatives to give orders, and so on. The immediate issue is: how do children go about learning this aspect of language use, and do children make a distinction between overt performatives (e.g., I *promise*) and implicit ones ([I assert])?

In 1967, Gruber presented a paper on the speech of one child recorded over a period of ten weeks, from age 1;3.[2] During this period, the child at first produced a number of complex utterances (composed of two or more words) that all related to her own needs and states, e.g., *Dory spoon, see flower, no my, want beads, Dory car* (see Gruber, 1973). This was established by careful analysis of the contexts of the child's utterances in the videotape records. In the tenth week, however, there was a marked change in that a number of complex forms were used that appeared to bear no relation to Dory's own state. Instead, she appeared to be making observations of fact about events and things around her. There was nothing discernible in the context from which one could infer that these utterances were self-based, as the earlier ones had been. This new type of utterance now contrasted with the old type, those utterances based

2. One year, three months.

on Dory's own needs and requests. On the basis of his analysis of use in context, Gruber concluded that those utterances relating to the child's own state were an elementary form of overt performative, equivalent to something like [I demand], while the other kind of utterance that emerged some two months later was what Gruber called a reportative. In the latter, the child was simply making an observation, unrelated to herself, about what she perceived, and was asserting that that was what she had noticed. The reportative was assumed to correspond to the covert form of performative underlying every speech act (Ross, 1970). Interestingly, the set of forms used by this child in the utterances designated as performative by Gruber all tend to refer either to the speaker (one of the obligatorily marked elements in the adult performative), e.g., *Dory* [her name], *I, me, my;* or to the addressee, using a vocative form, e.g., *mama*. The particular lexical item chosen to express the performative, e.g., *want, see,* simply reflects Dory's choice from among commonly heard forms from which she could infer the performative function (Gruber, 1973). On the basis of these data, Gruber suggests that children first use some sort of overt performative with the speech act function of indicating their own demands in all sorts of contexts, and that they will at first interpret their parents' utterances as performative in the same way regardless of their actual function. Later on, children begin to use reportative forms, distinguishing between their own demands related to personal comfort, etc., and their observations of others.

A similar analysis of a young child's two-word utterances is presented in Antinucci and Parisi (1973). Their subject, who is learning Italian as her first language, used only utterances with a request function to begin with. Like Dory's 'pure performatives', these tended to contain an element referring either to the speaker (e.g., *Claudia* [her own name], *me*) or the addressee (e.g., *Mamma*). These utterances, like Dory's, contained verbs that appear to have an overt performative interpretation for the child, e.g., *dai, tazie* [= give], *itto* [= see], *oio* [= want]. Later on, Claudia began to use what Antinucci and Parisi (1973) called 'descriptions'. These appear to coincide exactly with Gruber's reportatives.

Halliday (1975) presented a more detailed analysis of various functions that an utterance might have within the social context of language use. He also distinguished what he called pragmatic functions from mathetic functions. The child's first utterances all tend to fall into the pragmatic category, and relate to his own needs and demands of the instant, corresponding closely to the 'pure performative' or 'request' functions of the two other studies. The mathetic functions, which Halliday regards essentially as a learning device incorporated into language, represent the child's commentary on, and description of, what goes on around him. This appears to coincide fairly closely with the 'reportative' or 'descriptive' functions commented on by both Gruber and Antinucci and Parisi.

These approaches to language acquisition implicitly relate the acquisition of different sentence types and their possible functions to a theory of speech acts. This notion has also been implicit in a number of recent discussions. For example, Ervin-Tripp (1971) pointed out that 'Children's language development involves far more than grammar and phonology . . . children's developing skills include coming to say the right thing in the right way at the right time and place as defined by their social group' (p.37). This approach, with emphasis on the social function of speech, underlies Halliday's work, both in his analysis of function in English (e.g., 1970) and in his more recent analyses of the speech of a young child (1975). Dore (1973) has also proposed that language acquisition should be considered in the broader perspective of a theory of speech acts, including both overt performatives (Austin, 1962) and implicit ones (Ross, 1970), and taking into account the speaker's intention in saying something (Grice, 1967; Searle, 1970).

Even the preverbal child knows how to make his needs known through gestures and cries (Dore, 1973; Carter, 1973). Pointing at some object, for example, generally results in a parent getting it for the child; holding his hands above his head will often produce the (desired) effect of being picked up. Crying may have the function of asking for food, and so on. If the preverbal child already exhibits this range of functions (see also Ingram, 1971), then it is only natural that he should look for ways to express them verbally when he begins to use language. Dore presents some pilot data on two children at the one-word stage in support of his argument. His analysis is compatible with Halliday's (1975), despite the differences in terminology. Both Halliday (1975) and Dore (1973) also stress the importance of considering prosodic information as a clue to the functions the child assigns to different forms (cf. also Lewis, 1936; Crystal, 1973; Menyuk and Bernholtz, 1969).

The other aspect of social interaction that may play a role in learning about the functions of language is participation in dialogue. Lewis and Freedle (1973) looked at the proto-dialogues of parent and child pairs with children aged 12 weeks. As early as that, parent and child seemed to have established routines of interaction involving language on the parent's part to which the three-month-old would respond with vocalization. This kind of interaction may serve to set the child up very early on to attend to dialogue and its social function when he begins to use language proper. Halliday

(1973, 1975) suggested that dialogue serves a very important mathetic function for the child. Participation in dialogue is one way in which the child may actively learn in terms of eliciting 'new' words and finding out how to talk about events, people and objects. At the same time, the child is learning something about socialization in terms of the rules of conversation for talking to adults, to children, to friends and family, and to strangers (cf. Berko Gleason, 1973).

Grammatical relations
When the child first begins to use words with a recognizable semantic intent, he uses only single words. Therefore, even if the investigator assumes that the child uses these words holophrastically (McNeill, 1970), there is no reliable way to find out what grammatical role a particular word is playing on any specific occasion. The development of syntax has therefore been charted from the point at which the child begins to combine words, e.g., the change from an utterance consisting only of *baby* to forms like *baby sit* or *baby eat*. Much of the early work on children's syntactic structure attempted to do distributional analyses of the children's utterances from which to write rules of word combination that would produce the actual utterances in the corpus, plus others that were assumed to be possible, though non-occurring, combinations (e.g., cf. various articles in Bellugi and Brown, 1964). Initially, such structural analyses paid relatively little attention to the contexts in which the children had produced the utterances. However, the issue of whether the same combination of words always represented the same grammatical relations (i.e., meant the same thing) led investigators to pay much more attention to context and, as far as possible, to the child's intent in the analysis of his syntax (cf. especially Bloom, 1970). In fact, the increasing amount of attention paid to the context of the child's utterances was one factor (in addition to descriptive inadequacy) that led to the rejection of those distributional analyses known as pivot grammars (e.g., Braine, 1963); pivot grammars also lacked a way to account for the child's acquisition of the various grammatical relations (Bloom, 1971; Bowerman, 1973a).

The work of Chomsky, in particular, had a very strong influence on the later structural and theoretical framework with which many investigators approached the question of how the child's syntax developed. For example, Chomsky (1965) postulated that certain grammatical relations such as 'subject-of', 'predicate-of' and 'direct object-of' are universal across languages. McNeill (1966, 1970) proposed that the child's knowledge of such universal grammatical relations was innate, and would therefore influence the child's acquisition of language from the very first. Other investigators have simply assumed, in writing a grammar for a child, that relations like 'subject-of' and 'predicate-of' were functional for the child by the two-word stage of language development (e.g., Bloom, 1970).

Table 1

TWO-WORD UTTERANCES

A. Some examples of Pivot structures (Braine, 1963):

want + _____	want car, want get, want high, want jeep, want up
see + _____	see hot, see sock, see boy
all + _____	all broke, all buttoned, all fix, all wet
my + _____	my mommy, my milk, my daddy
no + _____	no bed, no down, no pee, no home
more + _____	more fish, more high, more read, more toast
_____ + *it*	do it, push it, move it
_____ + *off*	boot off, light off, show off, water off
_____ + *come*	mail come, mommy come
_____ + *do*	bunny do, daddy do, momma do

B. Some examples of grammatical relations (Bloom, 1970):

mommy sock	Subject + Object (Mother puts K's socks on K)
mommy sock	Genitive (Possessor + Object) (K picks up mother's sock)
sweater chair	Subject + Locative
eating cereal	Verb + Object

In contrast to those approaches, Schlesinger (1971, 1974) proposed that the stuctural relations found in children's early utterances are probably reflections of concepts like Agent and Action, rather than of the grammatical relations 'subject-of' and 'verb-of'. Indeed, such concepts are not necessarily specific to language at all since they form part of the child's cognitive system. The child acquiring language has to learn to map such concepts onto the surface structure of language; he does this, according to Schlesinger, via a set of 'realization rules' (Schlesinger, 1971).

Bowerman (1973b) took up the evidence for these two positions—innate grammatical relations (McNeill) versus relational concepts such as Agent (Schlesinger)—and showed that there was little support available at the moment for the innate arguments put forward by McNeill. For example, McNeill (1970) relied on the greater frequency of Verb + Object combinations over Subject + Verb combinations at the two-word stage in Brown's three children (Brown, 1973) to argue that frequency reflected the children's innate knowledge of the grammatical relation 'predicate-of'. The combination of Verb + Object formed a psychological unit, to which they would later attach noun phrases realizing the grammatical relation 'subject-of'. However, Bowerman's own data (1973a) showed a greater number of Subject + Verb combinations, from which one should logically argue that, for her three children, Subject + Verb was the psychological unit, to which 'object-of' was added later. Braine (1971) argued on slightly different grounds for the psychological reality of the relations 'subject-of' and 'predicate-of' to the young child. He pointed out that the majority of the 'replacement sequences' (see Table 2) he had recorded consisted of a short utterance with no subject, followed (immediately, or after probing) by the same utterance with the grammatical subject added. Bowerman (1973a, 1973b) also found replacement sequences in the corpora she collected, but she observed that the expanded version of the utterance as often involved the addition of a predicate to an original subject (e.g., *daddy . . . daddy already wash train*) or even of an object or a locative to a Subject + Verb sequence (e.g., *Immi draws . . . Immi draws there*). The only conclusion one can draw is that the frequency of certain types of two-word utterance (Verb + Object) and their occurrence in replacement sequences do not provide any clear evidence in favour of the innate grammatical relations argument (Bowerman, 1973b).

Table 2

REPLACEMENT SEQUENCES

A. Addition of Subject (from Braine, 1971):

chair . . . pussy cat chair
want that . . . Andrew want that
off . . . radio off
go nursery . . . Lucy go nursery
build house . . . Cathy build house

B. Addition of Predicate, of Direct Object or of Locative (from Bowerman, 1973b):

chick . . . chick sings
daddy . . . daddy wash . . . daddy . . . daddy already wash train
this belongs . . . this belongs here
Immi draws . . . Immi draws here
'lissa . . . 'lissa . . . 'lissa . . . 'lissa write
Kristin . . . Kristin sit chair
Kendall innere . . . Kendall innere bed

Bowerman herself (1973a, 1973b) suggested young children may only be using simple order rules for words that are assumed to fill various semantic functions. For example, she observed a strong tendency for initial noun phrases to be in an agentive relationship to the verb. The child, therefore, could be using an order rule—noun is followed by verb—to express the relation between the Agent and the Action initiated. In other words, 'children's initial efforts at word combination result from their discovery of ways to express various semantic relationships in the language they are learning' (Bowerman, 1973b, p. 210). Thus, the concept of the grammatical relation 'subject-of' would be a later development when the child eventually realizes that nouns with different semantic roles are treated in the same way with respect to different classes of verbs, i.e., they fill the same position (preceding the verb) and are affected in the same way by the various transformational possibilities in different sentence types. At this point, then, the child can make a higher order abstraction and come up with the more abstract notion 'subject-of'.

Bloom (1970) made no claims about the innateness of grammatical relations; she simply assumed they were functional for the children whose speech she was analysing. More recently, she has adopted the position that in the period prior to syntax (i.e., before the appearance of combinations of words) the child has to discover regularities in his experience and represent these in some way as conceptual relations between people, objects and events (Bloom, 1973). She suggests that children 'make certain cognitive distinctions first and proceed to analyse the speech they hear in relevant nonlinguistic contexts on the basis of such prior distinctions' (Bloom, 1973, p. 131). Bloom suggested that the underlying cognitive distinctions of Agent, Location, Action, and so on, are mapped onto the semantic roles or cases that underlie grammatical relations (cf. Fillmore, 1968). This approach is somewhat similar to those put forward by Ingram (1971) and by Greenfield and Smith (1976) in their analyses of the one-word stage. The analysis in context of the roles of single words that Greenfield and Smith present is very close to Brown's (1973) discussion of a Fillmorean approach to the two-word stage. Brown also suggests the cognitive basis for linguistic distinctions needs to be explored in much more detail before one can come to any conclusions about what may be innate about language.

Inflexions
Although many languages depend on word order to some extent to mark grammatical relations, others depend on the grammatical

relations being marked by inflexions. These may take the form of prefixes or suffixes added to the word, or of prepositions or post-positions, or some combination of these. Further inflexions may be used to indicate gender agreement and number agreement, e.g., between adjective and noun, and/or noun and verb, depending on the language. Inflexions or separate particles may also be used to mark definiteness in the noun. Other 'function' words that have often been considered along with inflexions proper are dummy verb forms, used primarily to carry tense and aspect markers (e.g., *do* in English), auxiliary verbs (*be, have*), and modals (*can, may, will*).

There are a large number of observational studies from different languages that report on the acquisition of such inflexions (e.g., Rūķe-Draviņa, 1959/1973; Guillaume 1927/1973; Gvozdev, 1961; Grégoire, 1937, 1947; Leopold, 1949). One of the most extensive and careful studies of English is that by Roger Brown (1973). Brown analysed the acquisition of some 14 different morphemes in the speech of three children. He set a criterion of use in 90% of the contexts where the inflexion would be obligatory for the adult, and then used this criterion to assess the relative order of acquisition for each child. Among the morphemes studied were the inflexions for aspect (*-ing*) and tense (*-ed*) on the verb, plural and possessive on the noun, the uncontracted and contracted forms of the copula *be* and the auxiliary *be*, the definite and indefinite articles (*the, a*), and two locative prepositions (*in, on*).

Brown found that the rank order for acquisition of the 14 forms was very similar for the three children ($r = \cdot 80$). However, the frequency of such forms in the parents' speech did not appear to play much role in determining which inflexions appeared earliest. Although the rank order frequencies of the forms were highly correlated for the parents ($r = \cdot 73$), the correlation between order of acquisition and parental frequency was very low ($r = \cdot 26$). Brown's analysis showed that the best predictor of the order of acquisition was in fact the relative semantic complexity of the distinction being made by a particular morpheme. For example, a morpheme that marked a single semantic distinction, x, was consistently acquired before one that marked x *and* some other distinction, y, at the same time. Thus, the past tense morpheme *-ed* marks whether an event was [Earlier in time], while the third person singular present *-s* marks both [Number] and [Earlier in time], and will therefore be acquired later (see further Brown, 1973). Although the relationship between semantic complexity and order of acquisition has been pointed out before in relation to inflexions (e.g., Imedadze, 1960; Slobin, 1966b, 1973), very few studies have documented and analysed the relationship as rigorously as Brown's.

Other studies of inflexions have looked at the child's ability to produce appropriate forms, and have also tried to test comprehension of such forms. For example, Anisfeld and Tucker (1968) replicated the pluralization section of Berko's (1958) original study where inflexional endings were elicited by using nonsense syllables. She had argued that the child's ability to add the appropriate inflexional ending to mark past tense, say, in English demonstrated that the child had abstracted a rule enabling him to produce such forms even for words he could never have heard before. Anisfeld and Tucker (1968) added a recognition task in which five and six year old children were presented with a form that was either singular or else marked as plural by /-s/, /-z/ or /-iz/. In choosing plural forms, the children did best, surprisingly, on the forms in /-iz/, the form that was worst in production. The explanation for this is probably that the children were more certain that /-iz/ following another sibilant was a plural, since few, if any, singular words in English could end that way. In contrast, many English words that are singular in meaning end in /-s/ or /-z/, e.g., *purse, lens, race, cause.* The children might therefore be less sure that a form ending that way was actually plural. This, then, would be independent of their greater skill in producing the plural forms in /-s/ and /-z/. Anisfeld and Tucker also found that children showed a general preference for adding some element to the stem to mark plural, rather than subtracting something. Thus, they chose the longer of two nonsense words significantly more often as the plural form: e.g., *wafk-wafk**ren** was preferred over *wafk-wa**f**. These data argue for the inherent markedness of the plural compared to the singular (Greenberg, 1966).

Bogoyavlenskiy (1957/1973) carried out work with Russian children rather similar to Berko's. However, he was mainly concerned with whether children knew what meaning certain suffixes contributed to the word, and whether they were able to segment the suffix from the word when asked. He found that most of the children tested were well aware of the meaning of different augmentative and diminutive suffixes combined with words, although they were less sure of agentive ones. However, very few of these children (aged 5;0-6;0) could tell him which part of the word it was that changed the meaning from, say, *animal* to *big animal* (e.g., *lar* and *larënok*).

Although the child's comprehension of what different inflexions add to the word and sentence meaning is an important source of information, this issue has not received as much attention as the child's production of inflexions. The findings on the relation between semantic complexity and order of acquisition, however, promise to lead to more detailed consideration of comprehension.

Sentence types

Much more attention has been paid recently to the early emergence of grammatical relations in young children's speech than to the development of different sentence types. However, there have been a few studies of negative and interrogative structures, of some complement types, and of some relative subordinate clauses. Some of these studies will be discussed below.

Klima and Bellugi (1966) presented an analysis of the first few stages in the child's development of negative and interrogative structures, based on an analysis of the data from Brown's three children. They took as the end point the adult rules for negatives and interrogatives based on various transformational analyses, and looked at the gradual convergence of the child's structures with the adult ones. In presenting the data, they concentrated on the forms produced by the children, and not on what they understood. However, they did

Table 3

EXAMPLES OF INTERROGATIVE AND NEGATIVE STRUCTURES
(from Klima and Bellugi, 1966)

Interrogatives:	Negatives:
I. Fraser water?	no singing song
sit chair?	no fall
	no mitten
where kitty?	no play that
where milk go?	wear mitten no
what that?	
what doing?	
II. see my doggie?	no pinch me
Mom pinch finger?	book say no
where my mitten?	don't bite me yet
where me sleep?	don't leave me
what book name?	
what the dollie have?	that not O, that blue
why you smiling?	he not little, he big
why not he eat?	that no fish school
why not me drink it?	there no squirrels
you can't fix it?	he no bite you
this can't write a flower?	I no want envelope
	I no taste them

III. does the kitty stand up?
      does lions walk?
      did I saw that in my book?
      oh, did I caught it?
      are you going to make it with me?

      will you help me?
      can I have a piece of paper?

      where small trailer he should pull?
      where my spoon goed?
      what he can ride in?
      what you had?

      why the Christmas tree going?
      why he don't know how to pretend?
      which way they should go?
      how they can't talk?
      how that opened?

      can't it be a bigger truck?
      can't you work this thing?

Paul can't have one
we can't make another broom

I didn't did it
I don't want cover on it
You didn't caught me
Paul didn't laugh

I gave him some so he won't cry
Donna won't let go

no, I don't have a book
that was not me
I am not a doctor
I isn't . . . I not sad

this not ice cream
this no good
I not crying
he not taking the walls down

don't put the two wings on
don't touch the fish

I not hurt him
I not see you anymore

---

report that, at the earliest stage, children tended to ignore a negative within the sentence, e.g., *I told you not to touch* or *Don't touch it*, but seemed to pay attention if there was an external negative, e.g., **No**, *don't touch it*. The earliest negative forms produced by the three children in fact consisted of a sentence nucleus, either preceded or followed by a negative, e.g., *No mitten, Outside no.* Bellugi (1971) also observed that, in the early stages of the development of such structures, the children seemed to be constrained by processing limits. For example, if the child generally produced two- or three-word sentences, the sentences which were negated tended to be shorter. A similar phenomenon was observed with the development of interrogatives where the data suggest that the child could only deal with one operation at a time, e.g., preposing the interrogative in Wh questions at first could not be combined with inversion of the subject Noun Phrase and the auxiliary, even though the child regularly performed this inversion with *yes/no* questions (see further Bellugi, 1971; Brown, 1968).

Bloom (1970) distinguished three different semantic types of negation in children's early speech at the point where the negative structures tended all to have the form of a negative word (*no, not*) added to the sentence nucleus (Klima and Bellugi, 1966). Having observed the contexts in which negatives were first produced, she argued that children first used negative sentences to remark on the absence of an object (*non-existence* in Bloom's terminology); next this was extended to indicate *rejection* of something proposed or offered by the adult; and lastly to indicate *denial* of a proposition. A similar progression was reported by McNeill and McNeill (1968) in their study of a child acquiring negatives in Japanese. In Japanese, unlike English, though, there is syntactic marking of the possible semantic distinctions that may be made between different kinds of negation.

Klima and Bellugi (1966) related both the development of negatives and of interrogatives to the acquisition of auxiliary and modal verbs. These verbs are intimately bound to the placement of the negative particle in English (Klima, 1964) as well as to the inversion of subject and verb in questions. Modals and auxiliaries first appear in negative form (*don't, can't, won't*) only, and are used to mark utterances as negative. Later, they also occur in their positive form and, following that, are used with inversion of the subject in *yes/no* questions. Later still, inversion of subject and verb also occurs in Wh questions. By this stage, many of the children's negative utterances look indistinguishable in structure from the adult's, except, for example, there is no alteration of *some* to *any*, and some double negation persists in sentences beginning with a negative such as *no-one* or *nothing* (cf. Klima and Bellugi, 1966).

Wh question words appear to come in, in spontaneous speech, in the following order: first, children ask *what* and *where* questions, then *why* and *how*, then *who*, then *when*. Approximately the same ordering was found by Ervin-Tripp (1970) in her study of compatible and incompatible answers to questions. She found that, at first, most Wh questions were treated as if they meant *what* or *where*, but the children she studied gradually came to give appropriate answers to the different questions. *When* tended to be the most difficult question form, and Clark (1971a) found that some three-year olds still consistently interpreted it as if it meant *where*. Lastly, Brown and Hanlon (1970) used measures of syntactic difficulty, based on cumulative derivational complexity, in their study of the emergence of tag questions. They found that predictions of relative ordering for many of the forms were compatible with such a model, but, as Watt (1970) pointed out, use of a particular linguistic description as a psychological model is problematic when the linguistic description changes.

Eventually children learn to produce and understand numerous complex sentence types, and are able to deal with forms like *John wanted to go home, John wanted Bill to go home, John asked Bill to go home, John was given the book, Bill had the book fetched, The man Bill pointed out was leaning against the post*, and so on. These examples represent only a few of the structures in the adult repertoire, and the acquisition of only a few of these has actually been studied systematically. Limber (1973) describes some longitudinal data from three children, aged 1;6-3;0. He observed that from about age 2;6 onwards, children produced forms like *Do it how I do it, Can we do it when we go home?, I don't know who is it*, and *I show you what we got*. The general trend in the production of relative clause forms seemed to be: first, children used place and manner forms (*where* and *how*); next, relatives were attached to various 'empty' nouns such as *thing, one, kind*, etc.; and lastly, relative clauses were attached to common nouns such as *ball*. However, the latter forms were still rare at age 3;0. There was also one striking asymmetry in the distribution of relative clauses in general: they never occurred on the subject noun phrase of the sentence. Finally, these children tended not to use *who* or *what* as relatives; their earliest relative clauses have a zero morpheme, later replaced by *that*.

Brown (1971) looked at comprehension of relative clauses with 3;0, to 5;0 year olds; he varied the position of the clause (e.g., *The man who is wearing a hat is talking to a lady* versus *A lady is talking to the man who is wearing a hat*), the focus (whether the subject of the main clause was the subject or object of the embedded clause), and the form of the pronoun (*who, who*-deletion, *which* and *that*). Brown (like Sheldon, 1972) found no effect of clause position, but subject focus (i.e., where there was the same subject in both the main and the subordinate clause) was easier for children to understand than object focus. Sheldon (1972) found a similar effect of parallel function for both subject relatives and object relatives (see also Slobin and Welsh, 1973). Sentences like *The dog that jumps over the pig bumps into the lion* (where *the dog* is the subject of both clauses) or *The dog stands on the horse that the giraffe jumps over* (where *the horse* is the object of both clauses) are much easier to understand than sentences like *The horse that the pig stands on bumps into the dog* (subject/object) or *The pig bumps into the horse that jumps over the giraffe* (object/subject). Her sentence types also covered a larger number of possible functions than Brown's. Lastly, Brown (1971) found that the pronoun form used made a significant difference; *which* and *that* were much easier than either *who* or what Brown called *who*-deletion, i.e. a zero morpheme.

Clark (1970, 1973a) analysed 3;0 year old children's spontaneous descriptions of events in time. The data showed that young children tended to begin by using temporal subordinate clauses only in second position, i.e., right-embedded. This applied to all clauses introduced by *when*, *if*, and *because*, the three most frequently used conjunctions, as well as to other conjunctions when the children first began to use them. At a later stage, children would also prepose subordinate clauses where the context called for it. Some conjunctions, such as *before* and *after*, tended to be used adverbially prior to their use as conjunctions. Also, *before* and *first* appeared to be more frequent in the protocols than *after* and *last* (Clark, 1970). Despite occasional spontaneous use of *before* and *after* as conjunctions, few children under 4;6 appear to understand these conjunctions in an adult manner (Clark, 1971a). Of the two, the conjunction *before* is interpreted correctly in a comprehension task at an earlier age than *after* (see also Ferreiro, 1971). The difficulty children have in comprehending instructions that contain these conjunctions seems to be quite independent of the main clause versus subordinate clause distinction suggested by Amidon and Carey (1972). A study replicating Clark (1971a) revealed that the differences between Clark's data and the Amidon and Carey data were an outcome of the actual task used in the latter study (see Johnson, 1975).

Aside from some work on elicited imitations and spontaneous production of some complex sentences (e.g., Menyuk, 1969), there has been comparatively little work on children's comprehension of more complex sentence types. Chomsky's (1969) study is one of the exceptions. She looked at comprehension of structures such as the following in 5;0 to 10;0 year-olds:

(1)   The doll is easy (hard) to see. [Who did the seeing?]
(2)   Donald promised Bozo to turn a somersault. [Who turned a somersault?]
(3)   John asked Bill what to do.[What did he say?]

Chomsky predicted that all three of these complement structures would be difficult for children to understand because they all violate the Minimal Distance Principle. This states that the Noun Phrase nearest the complement is the subject of the complement verb, as in:

(4)   Donald told *Bozo* to *turn* a somersault. [Bozo, you turn a somersault!]

Chomsky predicted that the children who had not yet grasped the syntactic constraints on complements following such verbs as *promise* would make systematic errors because they would assume that the Minimal Distance Principle applied to these verbs too. Her results showed that in general if the child correctly understood *ask* (question), he also knew *promise*, but not vice versa. All three complement structures were not mastered until age 9;0 or 10;0. Although Chomsky herself attributes the children's errors to lack of syntactic knowledge, it is not clear that one can really exclude all semantic factors. The questions asked of each child, designed to find out if he/she knew what *promise* meant, for example, did not constitute a rigorous test of the child's semantic knowledge (Clark, 1971b). Furthermore, one of Chomsky's main findings was that children systematically interpreted *ask* (question) as if it meant *tell*. In other words, they really did not yet know what that sense of *ask* meant.

Cromer (1970, 1972) followed up the first type of complement structure by Chomsky, the *easy* versus *eager* classes of adjectives; he used a larger number of adjectives from each class, and also included adjectives like *nice* which allow either interpretation depending on the context, e.g., *Children are nice to understand.* In this way, he was able to study some of the strategies children used at different stages in rather more detail. For example, the younger children nearly all used a primitive rule of equating surface subject with actor in sentences like *The wolf is hard to bite* as well as in sentences like *The wolf is happy to bite*. Chomsky's work on the complements of *ask* (question) versus *tell* has been followed up by Kramer, Koff and Luria (1972) who replicated the main results of her study. Kessel (1970) also replicated Chomsky's work, but claimed that the children he looked at achieved full mastery of *ask* (question), for example, much earlier than any of Chomsky's subjects. Kramer *et al.* (1972) pointed out, however, that Kessel failed to eliminate contextual cues that probably allowed appropriate guessing.

One important point about all these findings is that children clearly have a lot that remains to be learnt at age 5;0, the age once considered as the termination point in language acquisition. Aside from these studies, there has been comparatively little work on the more complex sentence-types that children have to acquire. The older literature, though, includes a number of survey studies, based on collections of speech samples from children at different ages. These studies provide some guidance to the kinds of sentence types that may be in the child's repertoire at different ages (cf. references in McCarthy, 1954).

SEMANTIC DEVELOPMENT

One aspect of semantic development that has already been discussed is the acquisition of case roles such as Agent, Location, and so on, that underlie grammatical relations. However, the child also has to start to deal with the assignment of meaning to words. In the course of acquiring language, he has to learn exactly what meaning the adults around him attach to particular lexical items. The child obviously starts with a handicap: he lacks the adult's experience of the world, of social constraints, and of linguistic communication. What he has in common with the adult is that he is a member of the same species, and hence possesses the same biological structure with which to process information. In the course of his first year of life, the infant spends most of his time taking in and organizing information about his surroundings. This provides a basis upon which to start constructing a dictionary of lexical entries once he begins to attach some consistent meaning to particular sequences of sounds.

Recent work in semantic theory has characterized meaning in terms of semantic components or features of meaning; it is combinations of such components that make up the meanings of words. The first of three parts of this section will consider this approach to the acquisition of lexical meaning. In the second part, I will go into studies of the child's knowledge of words whose meanings are related. Within linguistics, sets of related words are known as semantic fields. Several recent developmental studies have looked at how the child structures such fields, and how soon he realizes certain terms are related in meaning. In the last part, I will consider several studies of terms that refer to relations between objects (e.g., *above, in*) and to relational properties of objects (e.g., *wide, tall*). Throughout this section, it will be apparent that, just as it may be rather difficult to draw a line between what is syntactic and what is semantic within language, it is also hard to draw a line in many instances between what is word meaning and what is cognitive knowledge. This issue is not a new one, and indeed it continues to be a source of problems for semantic theory (cf. Bolinger, 1965). The overlap between semantic knowledge and general (world) knowledge will simply be reflected in a certain amount of overlap between this section and the next which will deal with some of the relations between linguistic and cognitive development.

Early meanings

The meaning of a word is generally considered to be made up of a set of smaller units of meaning that have been variously called semantic markers, semantic components, meaning postulates, minimal units of meaning, and so on (e.g., Katz and Fodor, 1963; Bierwisch, 1967, 1969). Both Postal (1966) and Bierwisch (1967, 1970) have suggested that underlying all languages, there is a universal set of semantic primitives; in addition, each language has a set of combination rules for combining primitives into clusters that then constitute the meaning of particular lexical items in that language. Languages may differ from each other, therefore, in the rules of combination used, but they all draw from the same set of semantic primitives. Furthermore, the semantic primitives are assumed to bear a fixed relation to the outside world which is determined by the biological structure of *homo sapiens*.

Bierwisch (1967) pointed out that such semantic primitives or semantic features would not actually represent the external physical properties of objects perceived or imagined, but rather the interpretations made of such properties by the human being. They are thus an integral part of the mechanisms of perception and conceptualization:

This then leads to the extremely far-reaching, plausible, hypothesis that all semantic structures might finally be reduced to components representing the basic dispositions of the cognitive and perceptual structure of the human organism. (Bierwisch, 1970, pp. 181-2)

This was one of the basic assumptions behind my own hypothesis about the acquisition of meaning (Clark, 1973b). First of all, the components of meaning used by the child were assumed to be the same as some of the components used by the adult. Secondly, since the child's experience of the world as well as of language is so limited compared to the adult's, he will begin by only attaching one or two of the relevant components of meaning to a word as its lexical entry. The choice of 'relevant' components will be determined largely by the child's previous experience, and they may therefore consist primarily of percept-based information (Clark, 1974). For example, the child has at his disposal all the perceptual information about objects designated by the adult in the context of new words. Thus, the child could well simply take such properties as details of shape, size, texture, sound, taste and movement, as being the meanings of new words (see Clark, 1973b).

The diary studies of children learning a large number of different languages bear out the general hypothesis presented in Clark (1973b). In particular, most of the diaries contain evidence that children have only attached one or two components of meaning to their first words. Let us take as an example the child who has attached some meaning to the word *apple*. The child then proceeds to call a large number of objects from different adult categories by that word, e.g., plums, door knobs, round light switches, tennis balls, and so on. From this, it can be inferred that the meaning that child has for the word *apple* is something like 'SMALL (X) and ROUND (X)'. Obviously, this lexical entry[3] only coincides in part with the adult one for *apple*. The child therefore has to learn more about the meaning of the word *apple* before he can use the term just as the adult would. The phenomenon just described has been called *over-extension* because the child over-extends the word to cover more than the adult domain of use.

Aside from the numerous reports of over-extension in the diary literature, several investigators have also performed small naturalistic experiments that provide further evidence that the child's earliest lexical entries are only partial entries by adult criteria. For example, Stern (1930) found that his children had a general word for all four-legged creatures. When he showed them some schematic line drawings, they named them with the same word. However, some eight months later when Stern repeated his experiment, the children apparently failed to recognize what the schematic drawings represented, and refused to name them. Clark (1974) has suggested that this is because the components perceived in the drawings no longer coincided exactly with the features present in the children's lexical entries. Both Major (1906) and Perez (1892) reported similar investigations, and found the same thing as Stern. Interestingly, the period in which children produce such noticeable over-extensions is a fairly short one, rarely more than eight months or a year, somewhere between age 1;0 and 2;6. The point at which *what* and *where* questions begin to occur with great frequency in children's speech roughly coincides with the end of the over-extension period (Clark, 1973b). It is possible that this increase in children's questions marks the point at which they realize how to ask for the names of objects. Prior to this, they have known that *apple* was not really the right word for 'doorknob', say, but they would use it to refer to that object because it matches on the relevant dimension(s). Thus, many over-extensions may be the result of the children's not yet knowing how to ask for the names of things.

The over-extensions reported in the literature tend to fall into six main categories, based principally upon the perceptual feature(s) the child has picked out as the meaning of the word. Examples from these categories are shown in Table 4. The basis for the child's over-extensions could be characterized in terms of the child's setting up an hypothesis about what a new word means, and then deriving from

3. The term *lexical entry* will be used to refer to the meaning attached to a word. The lexical entry itself may change over time, i.e., the child's representation of the meaning may change, as the child learns more about the adult's meaning for that same word.

Table 4

SOME EXAMPLES OF OVER-EXTENSIONS
(based on Clark, 1973b)

Category	Lexical item	First referent	Extensions and over-extensions in order of occurrence
SHAPE	mooi	moon	→ cakes → round marks on window → writing on window and in books → round shapes in books → tooling on leather book covers → round postmarks → letter O
	nénin	breast, food	→ button on garment → point of bare elbow → eye in portrait → face of person in photograph
	buti	ball	→ toy → radish → stone spheres at park entrance
	kutija	cardboard box	→ match box → drawer → bedside table
	kotibaiz	bars of cot	→ large toy abacus → toast rack → picture of building with columns along front
SIZE	fly	fly	→ specks of dirt → dust → all small insects → his own toes → crumbs of bread → a toad
	pin	pin	→ crumb → caterpillars
	bébé	baby	→ other babies → all small statues → figures in small pictures and prints
MOVE-MENT	sch	sound of train	→ all moving machines
	ass	goat with rough hide on wheels	→ all things that move, e.g., animals, sister, waggon → all moving things → all things with rough surface
SOUND	fafer	sound of trains	→ steaming coffee pot → anything that hissed or made a noise
	koko	cockerel's crowing	→ tunes played on violin → tunes on piano → tunes on accordion → tunes on phonograph → all music → merry-go-round
TEXTURE	bow-wow	dog	→ toy dog → fur piece with animal head → other fur pieces without heads
	wau-wau	dogs	→ all animals → toy dog → soft home-slippers → picture of old man dressed in furs
TASTE	cola	chocolate	→ sugar → tarts → grapes, figs, peaches
	candy	candy	cherries → anything sweet

that hypothesis a strategy for use of the word. For example, let us return to the child who has just heard the word *apple*. In attaching some meaning to this word, the child decides it must refer to objects that are relatively small and round. Therefore, whenever he wishes to obtain some object with those specifications, or to call adult attention to some object, he will use the word *apple* (or rather his phonological version of it). In learning to set adult-like limits on the boundaries of the category *apple*, the child will have to take negative adult feedback into account and add more features to his lexical entry for *apple* so as not to include tennis balls, paper weights and light switches. This feedback presumably takes several forms; first of all, the adult probably corrects noticeable over-extensions and secondly, often at the same time, the adult will provide the appropriate label, e.g., *That's not an apple, it's a ball.* Other feedback may not take the form of direct corrections given to the child, but may simply represent the adult's commentary on what the child is doing, what he is looking at, or what he experienced during that day.

Different stages of the over-extension process are well documented in several of the diary studies, save for one thing. It is not clear whether, when the child first hears a word, he immediately extends and, given the opportunity (i.e., exposure to appropriate objects), over-extends it, or whether there is a first stage in which he treats the word as if it was a proper name, and restricts it to one single object. The few cases of so-called under-extension (or over-restriction) reported in the literature suggest that some words are indeed treated like proper names. However, the problem is that this may happen simply because the child is not exposed to other possible instances (given his lexical entry) for some time, and therefore has little or no opportunity even for extension of the term, much less over-extension. None of the diary studies has been sufficiently detailed to provide answers on this issue.

Semantic fields

The child's task in assigning lexical meaning to words is a two-fold one: on the one hand, he has to decide what meaning a single lexical item has, and, if necessary, adjust his own initial meaning for it until it coincides with the adult one. On the other, he has to learn which words are also related to each other in meaning. For example, he has to learn what the words *get, receive, give, take, find* and *lose* mean, and also that they all relate to the notion of possession, and therefore have semantic components in common. Sets of words related in meaning are traditionally said to belong to the same 'semantic field' (Öhman, 1953; Lyons, 1968). Although there are a number of studies of the relations between terms that belong to the same semantic field (e.g., Bendix, 1966; Bierwisch, 1967; Fillmore, 1971), there have only been a few studies of this aspect of the child's lexical development.

The first semantic fields set up by the child might well be set up on the basis of some words having perceptual features from the same category present in their lexical entries. For example, the child might have several words for objects that moved. If a characterization of the kind of movement forms part of the lexical entry for each word, then the child might well treat these words as related. This would facilitate the addition of new words to the child's vocabulary, because the new word could be grouped with others already known. Presumably, such early structuring of the child's vocabulary would also have a facilitative effect on the memory structure being set up. The earliest vocabulary of young children seems to be very similar across children, and across languages. In a recent study of the first 50 words of several English-speaking children, for example, Nelson (1972) found that most children possessed some words for toys, vehicles, clothes, and food. The members of such categories could be grouped on the basis of the context within which they occur, are pointed out and described almost repetitiously by the adult for the benefit of the child learning to speak. The data from the diary studies show that percept-based factors probably play a very basic role in the child's earliest structuring of his vocabulary (Clark, 1973b, 1974). Objects are grouped according to similarity in some feature of shape or of movement, or some combination of such features, and then the child gradually learns to distinguish them at the lexical level by adding more features to his lexical entries. For example, many children start off with only one word for animals, which usually seems to have the meaning 'FOUR-LEGGED (X)', and is applied to dogs, cats, sheep, horses, goats, etc. As the child acquires other words for different animals, e.g. *baa-baa* or *lamb* in addition to *doggie*, he has to add more of the perceptual information he possesses to the lexical entries of both *doggie* and *lamb* in order to observe the adult category boundaries (cf. Clark, 1973b). Thus, the child probably begins to structure certain semantic fields very early on. Indeed, the setting up of such fields is an essential part of setting up lexical entries for the new words the child is in the process of acquiring.

The diary studies and more recent observational studies are dependent on the contextual cues to try to infer what kind of lexical entry the child has actually set up for a particular word. Production data, however, are not really at all reliable as a guide to the child's semantic knowledge at any particular stage. For example, the presence of several animal names in the child's repertoire is no guarantee that the child uses the semantic component Animate(x) in their lexical entries. To begin with, he may simply have entered some component relating to motion or to shape in representing the word meanings. The only experimental studies that have focussed on semantic fields have all involved slightly older children who were already at a stage when they could be asked questions or given instructions that helped reveal the state of their semantic knowledge. These studies have dealt with three semantic fields: spatio-temporal relations, dimensional relations, and kinship terms, all three of which have been studied fairly thoroughly within linguistics (cf. e.g., Bierwisch, 1967; Leech, 1969; Wallace and Atkins, 1960; Romney and D'Andrade, 1964).

Clark (1972) looked at the child's knowledge of the antonym pairs that make up the field of dimensional terms (e.g., *big-small, tall-short, wide-narrow, deep-shallow*) and the field of spatio-temporal terms (e.g., *in-out, up-down, in front-in back, first-last*). The technique used was to elicit the pair to each word that was supplied by the experimenter. The child therefore had to be able to understand something of each word's meaning, and be able to produce a word that was opposite in meaning in order to give responses. Children between 4;0 and 5;5 clearly grouped together words belonging to the same semantic field even before they knew the full meaning of all the words in that field. This was shown by the regular pattern of substitutions that the younger children used in giving many of their responses. For example, the positive term *big* was substituted for *tall, long, high, old, thick, deep* and *wide*, while its negative counterpart, *small* or *little*, was substituted for *short* (in response to both *tall* and *long*), *low, narrow, thin* and *young*. Among the spatio-temporal terms, *up* was substituted for both *over* and *above*; *in front* for *ahead*, *before* and *first*, and so on.

The pattern of substitutions also revealed a distinct ordering among the different pairs within each field. The semantically simpler terms acted as substitutes for more complex ones, but not vice versa. The substitutions therefore appeared to reflect the order of acquisition of different pairs of terms, where the order was determined by relative semantic complexity. For example, among the dimensional adjectives, the pair *big-small* is the simplest semantically because it may apply to one, two, or three dimensions, depending upon the properties of the object referred to. *Tall-short* and *high-low,* in contrast, refer only to a single dimension that is further specified as being vertical. The other dimensional terms refer to non-vertical dimensions, e.g., *long-short, wide-narrow, thick-thin* and *deep-shallow.* The three latter pairs are also further specified in that they are not used to refer to the most extended dimension of an object. Thus, the surface of a table is described as *long* and *wide*, a door as *high*, *wide*, and *thick*, and so on (Bierwisch, 1967). It was the semantically simplest pair of terms—*big-small*—that appeared in the majority of the substitutions (Clark, 1972).

Within the field of kinship terms, there have been several studies of what children know about parts of a particular kinship system, but until recently no one had investigated the system as a whole. Piaget (1928) included the terms *brother* and *sister* among the relational terms for which he elicited definitions from children at different stages of cognitive development. The different levels in the sophistication of the definitions provided have been replicated by Elkind (1962) and by Danziger (1957). The latter also looked at three additional terms: *daughter, uncle,* and *cousin,* and found essentially the same kinds of definitions there as well. At the first stage, children give definitions like *A brother is a boy.* Prior to this, they may pick up some irrelevant factor such as clothing, a name, hair, etc. The second level definitions usually recognized that there had to be more than one child involved, but reserved the word *brother* or *sister* for only one of the two. Finally, the child realized that the term *brother* involved a reciprocal relationship. Although the different levels of definition from Piaget's study can be characterized as different stages in the acquisition of the meaning of the words *brother* and *sister* (Clark, 1973b), none of these studies provides any information on whether one kin term is learnt later than another. Danziger (1957), who also considered some terms other than *brother* and *sister*, indicated that the definitions of different kin terms given by a single child were not all at the same level of sophistication, but he did not report any details of the differences found.

Haviland and Clark (1974) were concerned with the question of whether there was any order of acquisition comparable to that within the field of dimensional terms, based on differential semantic complexity. They therefore worked out an analysis of the fifteen main kinship terms used in English (*mother, father, son, daughter, brother, sister, grandmother, grandfather, grandson, granddaughter, uncle, aunt, niece, nephew, cousin*) from which to derive a semantic complexity metric. The differences in semantic complexity were used to predict the order of acquisition for the fifteen terms. Simpler terms should go through the different levels of definition found by Piaget earlier than more complex ones. Thus, there should be a negative correlation between the complexity of a kin term and the sophistication of the child's definition for that term. Overall, the predictions about semantic complexity were all borne out. The simpler a kin term was semantically, the earlier on the child could produce a near adult definition of its meaning. At the same time, there were clearly some other factors that probably interact with semantic complexity, e.g., the child's own sex and the child's 'viewpoint' as a child rather than as an adult (Haviland and Clark, 1974). Surprisingly, there was only a very low correlation between the sophistication of the child's definition and his personal experience with the kin relationship named. The children tended to give higher level definitions for terms of their own sex, and also gave higher level definitions for relationships they could hold to others (e.g., *brother*) than for those they could not hold (e.g., *grandfather*). The technique used—the elicitation of definitions— is, of course, open to the same criticisms as production data in general. It is possible that the relationship between semantic complexity and order of acquisition might be revealed in more detail from testing children's comprehension of meanings of different kin terms, instead of relying on the child's willingness to give definitions.

Relational terms
Relational terms that involve the comparison of two or more items or quantities have long been used in research on the development of conservation. However, few studies had considered whether the child really understands these terms in the same way as the adult prior to the work by Donaldson and Balfour (1968). In their study, Donaldson and Balfour showed 3½-year olds two apple trees, on each of which one could hang up to six apples. The trees were shown either with the same number of apples or with different numbers, and the experimenter then asked various questions about the relative amounts on the trees (e.g., Does one tree have more/less apples on it than the other?). Each child was then asked to point out which tree had more or less, or else to alter the relative state of one tree to the other (e.g., Make it so this tree has more/less than that one). All the children answered the first questions with no hesitation, but when asked to pick the tree with more or less, or to change the state of one tree, they gave correct responses only to *more*. The word *less* consistently elicited incorrect responses, in that instructions containing *less* were all treated as if they had contained the word *more*. Palermo (1973) replicated this study in detail, both with discrete items (apple trees) and with continuous quantities (water). In addition, Palermo carried out a second experiment on children aged 5;0, 6;0 and 7;0, and found that even a certain percentage in these age groups (e.g., 19% of the seven year olds) still treated *less* as if it meant *more* in a variety of different situations.

Donaldson and Wales (1970) reported on a further series of studies related to the work on *more* and *less*. The same children took part in several classification tasks in which they were asked to give the experimenter an object that was 'the same in some way' or 'different in some way' compared to the standard picked out by the experimenter. The results of this task are reminiscent of the children's behaviour with *more* and *less*: the children nearly always picked an object that was the same whether asked to pick one that was the same or different. In effect, *different* seemed to be interpreted as if it meant *same* (see further Donaldson and Wales, 1970). These children were also tested on their comprehension of the superlative and comparative forms of a number of dimensional adjective pairs, e.g., *biggest-wee-est, bigger-wee-er, longest-shortest, longer-shorter,* etc. In general, they tended to respond correctly more often when the adjective used referred to the positive (most extended) end of the dimension. This preference for positive pole adjectives in comprehension was also reflected in production: children consistently used positive pole adjectives rather than their negative counterparts, e.g., *long* rather than *short*. H. Clark (1970), in his discussion of their paper, pointed out that most of the pairs of terms studied by Donaldson and Wales were unmarked-marked pairs (Greenberg, 1966). Such pairs have asymmetric uses in language; for example, the unmarked member of the pair is always used to refer to the dimension in measure phrases, e.g., *That post is seven feet high*; it also provides the neutral question, e.g., *How high is the roof?*; and it generally supplies the name of the dimension, e.g., *height*. *Low*, in contrast, cannot be used in measure phrases, appears only in questions which presuppose certain assumptions on the speaker's part (*How low is it?*), and cannot provide the overall scale name. These linguistic asymmetries led Clark to suggest that the child first uses such terms as *more* and *less* in a nominal, non-comparative, sense. Thus, *more* and *less* both refer to something like 'quantity' or 'amount'. Then, since the unmarked (nominal) term refers to extension rather than relative lack of extension, the child begins to use both *more* and *less* to refer to the extended end of the dimension (i.e., greater amount). Lastly, he learns that the terms *more* and *less* actually contrast, and that *less* means lesser amount. Palermo's (1973) study shows that the last stage in learning what *less* means, in fact, may not be attained until age 7;0, although most children probably learn it a bit earlier than that.

Some other recent studies of relational terms have concentrated on the acquisition of the meaning of certain conjunctions. For example, Clark (1971a) studied children's interpretations of the temporal conjunctions *before* and *after*. Three-year olds did not understand either term, and used the strategy of simply ignoring the words when asked to carry out instructions. As a result, they would act out two-part instructions in the order in which the two events were mentioned. At the next stage, children had learned what *before* meant, but still used order of mention with *after*. Next, some children went through a stage of treating *after* as though it meant the same as *before*, a result analogous to that found in the *more-less* data, and finally, near age 5;0, some of the children realized that *after* was actually the opposite of *before*. Ferreiro (1971) found exactly the same results independently, in her work on temporal relations with French-speaking children.

Many verbs and nouns are also relational in nature. For example, kin terms refer to a relationship between two or possibly more people. Thus, the word *aunt* in English designates the sister of one's father or mother, or the spouse of one's mother's brother or of one's father's brother. Acquisition of the relational component itself, with recognition of its reciprocity, comes later than acquisition of features like Male(x) or Female(x) (cf. Haviland and Clark, 1974; Clark, 1973b). With verbs, the relationships are those between the different case roles that are allowed with the verb. For example, *drive* may take an Agent, e.g., *He was driving*, and an Object, e.g., *He was driving the car*. The verb *see* marks the relation between the Experiencer who does the seeing, and the entity perceived, e.g., *He saw the falcon*, and so on (Fillmore, 1968). However, aside from the investigations of the child's production of certain case relations (e.g., Brown, 1973), and his eventual derivation from them of grammatical relations like subject-of (Bowerman, 1973b), there has been very little work on the child's acquisition of different verb meanings.

One of the few studies that bears on this question is Chomsky's (1969) work (see above, p. 18). Her data can be interpreted as showing that children aged 5;0 and over have not yet learnt exactly which roles go with certain verbs. For example, part of the meaning of *promise* is that the person giving the promise puts himself under an obligation to do whatever was promised (Clark, 1971b; Searle, 1970). A rough performative analysis can also be made of the two verbs *tell* and *ask* (question), such that in imperative contexts, e.g., *Tell John to come here*, *tell* has the meaning 'I order you—you say to X—S' where S is the complement sentence. *Ask* (question), however, has a much more complex semantic structure: 'I order you— you say to X—you request X—X say to you—S'. Since there is overlap between these two lexical entries, *tell* is not unexpectedly used as a substitute until the child acquires the more complex semantic structure of *ask* (cf. Clark, 1973b).

These studies of relational terms, however, merely provide a glimpse of the complexities that the child has to deal with in setting up lexical entries for various complex terms. While these data, together with the semantic field data, provide some strong evidence that the more complex a term is semantically, the later it will be acquired, singularly little is known, at this point, about the relative complexity of different terms.

COGNITION AND LANGUAGE

The growing interest in semantic factors in language acquisition has also led to people taking a closer look at the kinds of cognitive abilities children bring to the task of acquiring language, and at the kinds of knowledge the child might have acquired prior to language acquisition. Research on cognitive development has always been somewhat concerned about how language might affect cognition or vice versa (e.g., Sinclair-de Zwart, 1967, 1969), but few investigations considered whether the child really understood the instructions he was given in exactly the same way as the adult. For example, most conversation tasks require that the child understands the meanings of several relational adjectives, e.g., *bigger-smaller, taller-shorter, longer-shorter*. The child will also be asked to make judgements of *more* and *less, same* and *different*. In the light of the studies of semantic acquisition, it is clear that failure on certain tasks may simply reflect a failure to understand the words in the instructions.

In the era of syntactic studies, when a great deal of language was assumed to be 'given' via certain, hitherto unspecified, innate mechanisms specific to language, very few researchers tried to integrate language with other aspects of cognitive development. However, several observations on the part of researchers into language acquisition have led to some changes in outlook. First of all, it was noticed that children learning very different languages produced utterances that looked extraordinarily alike during the early stages. While such similarities could be put down to the existence of an innate capacity for language that is manifested in the same way, regardless of the language being learnt, a number of investigators have gone further. They have begun to try to specify what specific strategies the child might bring to the task of learning language, and to look for evidence for or against the use of various strategies that have been posited. Such strategies are assumed to operate both on output—the child's own spontaneous utterances—and on input—the child's interpretations of what is said to him.

The second observation that has led investigators to look more closely at the cognitive basis for language acquisition is that children display considerable consistency in the order in which they acquire certain linguistic distinctions (e.g., Brown, 1973; Slobin, 1973). This has been found true for children learning the same language, but it would also appear that some distinctions are easier than others across languages too. In such instances, the easier distinctions are acquired earlier. The question this raises is whether the complexity of semantic distinctions is actually based on some underlying cognitive complexity that has been encoded linguistically. The problem is to find a way of assessing cognitive complexity independently of language in order to find out what role complexity plays in language acquisition in general.

Operating principles
The child that constructs a grammar for his first language has first to be able to 'cognize the physical and social events which are encoded in language, and [has to be able to] process, organize and store linguistic information' (Slobin, 1973, p. 176). Slobin (1973) is concerned both with the order of acquisition of certain linguistic distinctions and with the child's strategies for organizing the language input that he receives. He takes as given what might be called 'language-definitional' universals, for example, that all languages have a general communicative function, and as such serve to express assertions, orders, denials, requests, and so on. In considering the child's strategies, Slobin starts from the point where the child has already recognized that words have meaning, and that words can be combined to form meaningful utterances. These combinations may be marked in a number of ways, dependent in part on the language, in order to express grammatical relations, tense, mood and aspect, and so on. The main devices that the child has at his disposition are inflexional markers (e.g., the case endings used to mark the different grammatical roles in a language like Russian or German), prepositions or postpositions (as used in English and Turkish), and word order.

Slobin's argument goes as follows. The regular order of acquisition observed for many linguistic distinctions both within and across languages occurs because the acquisition of such distinctions is dependent on prior cognitive development. If a child has not yet developed the underlying conceptual distinction, he will be unable to map it onto a particular linguistic form. It is therefore the relatively fixed order of acquisition of conceptual distinctions that governs the order of acquisition of linguistic distinctions. In both instances, the simpler distinctions are the ones acquired first. However, the child may mark a distinction such as plurality some time before he learns the appropriate adult forms of marking. For example, English-speaking children tend to mark plurality by using *more* or some numeral, as in *more shoe, two shoe,* or occasionally by using reduplication, as in *shoe-shoe.* These forms are taken to mark the appearance of the conceptual distinction. A few months later, the child begins to use the (adult) plural inflexion, *-s.* Slobin proposes that the gap between the appearance of the conceptual distinction and the use of the adult marking for that distinction is an indication of the degree of formal complexity involved in making that distinction in that language. Thus, plurality in Arabic is formally much more complex than plurality in English because children do not master the adult system until age 10 or 12 (Omar, 1970). Notice that such a measure of formal linguistic complexity will vary across languages with the distinction being marked, and will be relatively independent of the kind of linguistic description provided by a grammar of the language.

The test of Slobin's proposal requires detailed investigation of the kinds of devices used by young children to make different linguistic distinctions, the order of appearance of such devices, and the gap between appearance of some marking and the appearance of the correct adult forms. On the basis of his review of a large amount of cross-linguistic data, Slobin (1973) came up with several general operating principles that children appear to use both in production and in comprehension of language. These operating principles are stated in a very general form, e.g., *Pay attention to the ends of words* (p. 191), *Pay attention to the order of words and morphemes* (p. 197), *Avoid interruption or rearrangement of linguistic units* (p. 199), *Underlying semantic relations should be marked overtly and clearly* (p. 202), *The use of grammatical markers should make semantic sense* (p. 206). The evidence in support of each principle took the form of 'universals' of development that had been observed in children learning very different languages. For example, the universals observed in relation to the last principle mentioned above include the following:

Universal 1: When selection of an appropriate inflection among a group of inflections performing the same semantic function is determined by arbitrary formal criteria (e.g., phonological shape of stem, number of syllables in stem, arbitrary gender of stem), the child initially tends to use a single form in all environments, ignoring formal selection restrictions.

Universal 3: Semantically consistent grammatical rules are acquired early without significant error. (Slobin, 1973, pp. 206-7)

Each such universal is backed by diverse observations from both production and comprehension in relation to a variety of grammatical forms and sentence types.

Throughout his discussion, Slobin emphasizes the semantic distinctions that underlie and hence motivate many if not most of the grammatical distinctions made in language; these distinctions include a large variety of inflexions (e.g., in Russian, Finnish or Latvian) as well as agreement rules and word order rules. Wherever there is a clear relationship between the distinction being made and a single inflexion, the child finds it relatively simple to learn, e.g., Hungarian locative relations each marked by a single, invariable suffix on the noun; but wherever there appears to be no direct relation between the semantic distinction and the means used to express it, the child will take much longer to express it in correct adult form, e.g., locative relations in Serbo-Croatian which are marked both by prepositions and case markers which rarely correspond in a one-to-one fashion to designate a unique relation; for example, the same preposition combined with different suffixes marks different distinctions, and the same suffix does not consistently mark the same relation. As Slobin points out, the difference in formal complexity between Hungarian and Serbo-Croatian in the expression of locative relations means that Hungarian is easier to acquire. This is clearly demonstrated in the case of some young bilingual children who consistently expressed locative relations when using Hungarian (e.g., *doll-drawer-in*) but failed to mark such relations in Serbo-Croatian (e.g., *doll drawer*).

Bever (1970a, 1970b) stressed that the study of structure in children's language, in isolation from the rest of cognitive development, was far too narrow an approach to language acquisition. He further pointed out that 'Certain ostensibly grammatical structures may develop out of other behavioral systems rather than being inherent in grammar' (1970a, p. 280). Bever then discussed various modes of processing information and proposed that certain basic perceptual strategies are used by both adult and child in the segmentation of language and in the assignment of grammatical relations to sequences of words. One of these strategies was based on the principle: *Any Noun-Verb-Noun (NVN) sequence within a potential internal unit in the surface structure corresponds to 'actor-action-object'* (1970a, p. 298). Use of this principle, for example, would account for the fact that young children tend to interpret reversible passives incorrectly because they always assign the role subject-of to the first noun (e.g., Slobin, 1966a; Sinclair and Ferreiro, 1970). Another of Bever's strategies resembles Slobin's operating principle that grammatical markers should make semantic sense: *Constituents are functionally related internally according to semantic constraints* (1970a, p. 296).

Bever's principles mostly deal with segmentation of units at the clausal or sentential levels while Slobin's emphasize the segmentation that has to operate at the word level when the child is still at the stage of learning to interpret and use inflexions, prepositions and postpositions. Secondly, Bever was not as concerned with how such strategies might originate. He did suggest, however, that they might be formed in response to natural probabilities in the actual speech that the child is exposed to. Thus, they would presumably result from the child's selective inductions from earlier linguistic experience. However, other investigators have argued that the child's first inductions about linguistic relations are more probably based on previous non-linguistic experience with objects, actions and events. Regularities in these experiences would then form the basis for looking for a mapping between the parental utterance in a certain routine context (e.g., feeding or changing) and the relationship (e.g., actor-action) that was perceived (cf. Bloom, 1973; MacNamara, 1972).

Cognitive complexity
Slobin's (1973) proposal that 'The rate and order of development of the semantic notions expressed by language are fairly constant across languages, regardless of the formal means of expression employed' (p. 187) was based on the hypothesis that the stages in cognitive development are universal, and that cognition sets the pace for language acquisition. The difficulty lies in determining the relative difficulty of the cognitive distinctions that can be expressed in language. Most investigators have tackled this issue from the linguistic end, and considered what the child produces in particular contexts at different stages (e.g., Bloom, 1973; Antinucci and Parisi, 1973). However, unless one knows exactly what meaning the child has attached to particular words, one might attribute to the child more knowledge than he actually has at that stage (Schlesinger, 1974).

On the other hand, the infant spends his first year or so actively taking in information about his environment, the objects in it, and the various kinds of events that can occur. It is therefore probable that the child has formed a number of expectations about the way things are around him by the time he comes to start work on language as a coding system. In trying to map his percepts and experience onto language, the simplest things to map will be those he already 'knows about' at the cognitive level. The similarities that have been observed across languages for the two-word stage would tend to back up Slobin's position that cognition exhibits universal stages of development, and that the child first looks for ways to encode what he already knows. For example, the functions of indicating the location of objects, of demanding and negating, questioning, and describing situations are all present at the two-word stage. Moreover, such utterances from different languages look very alike in structure (Slobin, 1970). The two-word stage, of course, does not mark the child's first attempts to match up his cognitive knowledge with language. This occurs at the one-word stage. However, it is very difficult to know how much to attribute to the child in the absence of any grammatical markers or use of word order to give a clue to the relationship being mapped. Greenfield and Smith (1976) have attempted to look at single words in the context of the situation in which they were uttered, and infer from the context what function the word had. While they found that the two children they observed seemed to go through distinct stages in the expression of different functions, it remains very difficult to know whether the child had interpreted the situation in the way the adult *assumes* it was interpreted.

There is some evidence for expectations about normal roles, functions and orientations of naturally occurring objects in the literature on perceptual development (e.g., Ghent, 1960; Ghent Braine, 1972) as well as in some recent work on semantics (Clark, 1973b, 1974). Ghent, for example, found that children below the age of about 5;0 had difficulty in matching an object that had been rotated 90° or 180° from the vertical to a normally oriented, vertical counterpart. In Clark (1974) it is proposed that the child actually starts out with certain hypotheses about the basis upon which to categorize objects and relations. These hypotheses take the form of assigning as word meanings whatever perceptual characteristics the child has abstracted as the probable meaning. For example, he might assume that the word *apple* means 'SMALL(X) and ROUND(X)'. From this hypothesis, the child derives a strategy for the use of this word, namely that any object for which he has no other name already that fits the two criterial features of *apple* can be referred to as an *apple*. From this vantage point, it is clear that there is a very close link between the child's developing cognitive system that interprets all input and the semantic (linguistic) system that the child is acquiring. The semantic system, like the perceptual one, has to be interpreted at the cognitive level in order for the child to make use of the information given. Thus, in going from perceptual information to language, or vice versa, there has to be a way of mapping one system onto another. Closer examination of the linguistic system and its emergent semantic structure may provide more insight into the exact nature of these mapping operations.

The child's preliminary hypotheses about meaning, however, may not accord with the adult configurations of semantic components that make up the lexical entries of certain words. Since, in such instances, the child will have to learn *not* to use the strategies he has derived for particular words, his acquisition of the meanings of such words might be regarded as being more complex cognitively. The simpler word meanings will be those where the outcome of the child's strategies coincides more closely with the adult meaning. The relative distance between the child's strategy and the adult meaning, therefore, might be used as a measure of the cognitive complexity of acquiring different linguistic distinctions. For example, suppose the child only knew that *more* and *less* referred to Amount(x) but he also had a strategy of choosing the larger or more extended among any set of objects. The combination of such partial semantic knowledge and the strategy will result in 'correct' responces to *more*, and 'incorrect' ones to *less* (see Clark, 1973c).

From the cognitive point of view, the data on children's early word meanings and the over-extensions reported show how actively the child depends on his prior experience and perceptual knowledge when he tries to map language onto what he already knows. Furthermore, some cognitive mechanisms may make it easier for the child to learn certain linguistic distinctions because the child's hypothesis and the derived strategy happen to coincide with the adult word meaning. One situation in which a linguistic asymmetry might be attributed to an underlying cognitive asymmetry is that of polar adjective pairs. Children are widely reported to learn positive dimensional adjectives, e.g., *big, tall*, that refer to extension along some dimension, before they learn the negative terms referring to relative lack of extension, e.g., *small, short* (see above p. 26). When young children were given a concept-learning task using nonsense syllables (constructed from Consonant plus Vowel plus Consonant sequences) to name the ends of certain dimensions, they consistently learnt the meaning of the CVC for relative extension on the dimension more quickly than the one for relative lack of extension. Because the children were not exposed to any of the linguistic asymmetries in the case of the nonsense syllables, Klatzky, Clark and Macken (1973) suggested that it was possible that the asymmetry between positive and negative adjectives in language is in part the result of an asymmetry at the cognitive level in the processing of relative extension versus relative lack of extension. This same asymmetry could be the underlying factor in the differences for positive and negative adjectives in adult processing (e.g., H. Clark, 1969). More generally, it might even be plausible to argue that the asymmetries in the occurrence and usage of positive and negative adjectives across languages (Greenberg, 1966) are ultimately based on cognitive factors.

The problem of mapping language onto what the child already knows is an all pervading one, and has to be tackled for every domain that can be discussed in linguistic terms. In most instances, it is necessary to lay out what the child might know from the perceptual point of view, and then look at how such information might be mapped onto the linguistic structure available in a particular language. H. Clark (1973) looked at the possibilities for mapping from perceptual space, to the kinds of spatial relations encoded in English. He pointed out that human perception of space is organized along Euclidean lines, largely because of how the eyes, ears and other perceptual apparatus are organized for humans. The perceptual organization of space should influence the child trying to interpret the linguistic system. He should find it easiest to map percept and word meaning wherever these coincide, and harder where there is no one-to-one match between the perceptual information and the linguistic meaning.

This approach is assumed in some recent work on the acquisition of the meanings of locative terms like *in, on* and *under*. Clark (1973c) found that children aged 1;6 used certain non-linguistic strategies only, when asked to carry out instructions containing these locatives. The strategies appeared to be based on the child's knowledge of the expected spatial relation between two objects. One of these strategies, for example, could be verbalized as: 'If *y* is a container, *x* is inside it'. Regardless of whether the instruction contained the preposition *in* or *on*, therefore, the young child always placed *x* inside when *y* was a container. This strategy was quite appropriate when the instruction contained *in*, so the child did not have to unlearn anything with respect to that lexical item. With *on*, though, the child has to learn not to apply this 'container' strategy even when *y* is a container. *On* is therefore learnt later than *in* because the word meaning does not coincide directly with the child's prior perceptual organization. Since the acquisition of the meaning of *on* requires that the child learn *not* to apply his primitive non-linguistic strategy, it is more complex cognitively. In other words, the cognitive complexity of different semantic distinctions within the language could be viewed as the interaction between the child's organization of his prior cognitive and perceptual knowledge and the degree to which this can be mapped directly onto the linguistic system he is trying to acquire.

PHONOLOGICAL DEVELOPMENT

From the earliest point in life, the normal child is exposed to the sounds of speech used by the adults around him. It is from this auditory input that he has to learn to segment out similar sequences and relate them to the situation in which they occurred. In discussing the child's approach to the syntax and semantics of his language, it was taken for granted that he had sorted out how the sound system worked, i.e., that a relatively limited number of sounds could be combined in certain ways in order to form strings that had meaning in that particular language. The task of segmentation at this level, however, is by no means a simple one.

First, the child has to come to the realization that certain sounds have a distinctive function in the language he is exposed to, while others may be ignored. For example, the child learning English need not pay any attention to aspiration with voiceless stops because aspiration does not have a distinctive function. The child, though, is not really in a position to assume this until he has actually worked out what the whole system is. In learning which sounds do have distinctive functions, he has to pay attention to the sets of *oppositions* among sounds that occur in the adult's speech. For example, in English there is a series of voiced stops that contrast with voiceless stops. Their distinctive function shows up in such word pairs as *tip/dip, kill/gill*, and *pill/bill*. In addition to the sets of oppositions, the child has also to learn which sequences of sounds are possible (allowable) within that particular language, for example, that clusters like /gl-/ or /kl-/ can and do occur in English, but that /dl-/ and /tl-/ do not. Furthermore, certain sequences of sounds, within or across word boundaries may be modified in rapid speech, e.g., the devoicing of a voiced stop preceded by a voiceless consonant, as in *let's go* [lɛtsko ⊙].

While these changes may depend on rate and style of speech (e.g., casual versus formal), others involve regular patterns of alternation in the language. For example, the vowels in many words change when stressed, or when going from a stressed form to an unstressed one, as in the pairs *sincere-sincerity, oppose-opposition, opaque-opacity*, etc. A somewhat similar alternation in vowel form may be used to mark the past tense, e.g., *lead-led*, or the plural form, e.g., *woman-women*. Furthermore, different forms of the same morpheme may be regularly assigned to words on the basis of their phonological structure. Two cases that have been discussed earlier are the plural and past tense forms used with most English nouns and verbs. The plural morpheme has three different forms, /-z/, /-s/ and /iz/, used on nouns like *buds, bits* and *glasses*, respectively. The past tense morpheme likewise has three forms, /-d/, /-t/ and /-id/, as in *jabbed, rushed* and *fitted*. The choice of such forms is determined by the phonological shape of the final segment in the word to which the ending has to be added.

The child also has to master the suprasegmental features of the phonological system, e.g., word stress, sentence stress, intonation contours and the different communicative functions of such contours.

The present section will consider some of the data and theories pertinent to the acquisition of the phonological aspects of language, first in terms of what the child himself produces at different stages, and secondly in terms of what he appears to pay attention to and treat as meaningful in the course of acquisition.

Order of acquisition

The child begins to vocalize fairly early on in life, but he does not come to use sequences of sounds with any consistent semantic content, e.g., begin to speak, until sometime between twelve and twenty-four months. To begin with, the infant produces a basic rhythmical crying sound, characterized by Wolff (1966) as consisting of a cry, a rest, breathing in, a rest and then another cry. This form of cry remains in the child's repertoire for about six months. It also occurs in slightly different forms to express apparent anger, with added loudness, and pain, with a longer crying portion. By the end of the first month, the infant begins to produce non-cry vocalizations as well. These display much greater variation in the temporal and frequency patterns, and involve greater use of the articulatory organs (Wolff, 1966). A third stage in the child's vocalization seems to begin at about four or five months old. It is at this point that the child begins to babble. The sounds produced appear to be more vowel-like and consonant-like, and are combined into syllable patterns with reduplication, e.g., *babababa*. At this stage, too, adult-like intonation contours are imposed on the child's babbling. These forms of vocalization continue for some six to eight months.

The last phase in this progression towards adult-like speech sounds usually begins sometime between nine and twelve months. Many observers have noted several changes that take place at this point. First of all, there seems to be a considerable reduction in the range of phonetic forms appearing in the child's repertoire. The small set of sounds remaining make up certain oppositions that are gradually elaborated so as to form more and more of the differentiations relevant to the particular language.

Secondly, the observations of many investigators suggest that there may be a sharp discontinuity between the babbling stage in vocalization and the onset of actual speech. This discontinuity is marked by the reduction in the range of phonetic forms available to the child, and may involve a brief period of minimal, or even no, vocalization, e.g., Jakobson (1941/1968). Other observers have claimed that there is no discontinuity, and that, furthermore, the babbling stage forms the basis for the later emergence of actual utterances. This dispute arises in part from the difference between the so-called linguistic approach to the issue (Jakobson, 1941/1968) and the learning theory approach (e.g., Mowrer, 1958). The latter stresses continuity between the stages of different vocalization, and accounts for the reduction in sound types produced by the child in terms of selective reinforcement by the parents of just those sounds that belong to the language being learnt. This approach, though, has no criteria for predicting and hence explaining the orderly nature of the distinctions that the child goes through after the babbling stage. Furthermore, parents do not appear to be selective in the kinds of sound they encourage, but simply respond to any vocalization (cf. Kaplan and Kaplan, 1970; Ferguson and Garnica, 1975). However, it is possible that certain aspects of language, such as intonation, do exhibit a continuity of development, while the development of segmental structure is independent of the babbling stage (cf., e.g., Lieberman, 1967).

Jakobson (1941/1968) proposed that there were two separate periods of phonological development. First of all, the child goes through a babbling stage during which he produces a wide range of different sounds many of which later disappear either permanently or for an extended period of up to several years. The sounds produced during the babbling period do not seem to appear in any particular order, and they also seem to be unrelated to later stages of development. The disappearance of many sounds formerly produced by the child signals the onset of the second main period distinguished by Jakobson. The second period dates from the point at which the child recognizes that certain sounds have a distinct linguistic value, and are used for designation. The earlier babbling stage may give way imperceptibly to the stage of phonological development proper, or else there may be an intervening silent period. Once the child has entered the second period, his phonological development follows a relatively invariant and universal order in mastering the various oppositions between the sounds of the language around him. The order in which children go through the different stages posited by Jakobson is determined by what Jakobson calls the principle of 'maximum contrast', such that 'development proceeds from the simple and undifferentiated to the stratified and differentiated' (Jakobson, 1968, p. 68). The more oppositions a sound enters into within a particular language, the more complex it will be to learn. Thus, the child in fact goes about constructing his phonological system in terms of the oppositions he can make at each stage, rather than in terms of the particular sound. This is obviously reasonable since one's knowledge about the possible contexts in which a particular *sound* could occur is dependent on knowledge of the system as a whole. And it is just this knowledge of the system as a whole that the child is trying to acquire. Thus, the child's emergent system has a structure of its own that corresponds in certain systematic respects with the adult one, even though the child might be using different sounds, e.g., *gogi* for *dog*, *ti* for *cat*, and so on.

After going through a large number of diaries of children learning different languages, Jakobson came to the conclusion that the order in which children go about learning phonological oppositions is predictable from what he called 'laws of irreversible solidarity', i.e., laws of implication that hold in the description of the phonological structure of languages in general. These laws are implicational in nature and take the form: *If a language contains Y, it will also contain X*; however, the presence of X in the language does not tell one whether that language also contains Y. These laws are derived from the study of the sound systems of many languages of the world, and the frequency with which particular phonemic contrasts appear within and across languages. Those oppositions that are found most generally across languages will be acquired relatively early, while those that are very rare will be acquired much later.

Jakobson deals only with the acquisition of segmental phonology, and leaves aside such things as stress and intonation. However, he also fails to discuss what may happen with respect to a particular opposition depending on its position in the word. The phoneme /p/, for example, can occur initially, medially or finally. Moscowitz (1970) found that the initial position is one in which there is maximum stability for consonants and also maximum contrast within the young child's system. In medial position, there is much more variability, and this position, in fact, seems to allow much more phonetic experimentation. Use of final position consonants is relatively rare in the developing system.

Moscowitz (1971) extended Jakobson's theory to deal in more detail with the syllabic structure of early word forms. In general, she took the position that once the child has acquired a certain amount of control over sentence intonation and can thus identify units at the sentential level (cf. also Lieberman, 1967), he can then turn his attention to the analysis of segmental material. Moscowitz (1971) placed great emphasis on the role of the syllable, and suggested that the child actually deals with oppositions at the syllabic level to begin with, rather than at the segmental level. The first syllable type used is CV, but as the number of such syllable-words used by the child grows, he also begins to elaborate the syllable structure and produce forms such as CVC, VC, and V.

Following this stage the child begins to produce reduplicated syllables as words, e.g., CVCV; it is at this point, where the syllable and the word become separable, that Moscowitz claimed that the child begins to analyse syllables in terms of their component segments. At first, reduplication involves identical syllables; later only the consonants or only the vowels are kept the same. Her analysis is backed by reference to a variety of previous studies that have reported on the early word-forms used by children learning several languages (cf. also Ferguson, Peizer and Weeks, 1973).

Waterson (1971) examined characteristics of utterances from an 18 month old child such as nasality, glottality, stop (complete closure), frontness, voicing, and labiality. The presence of one such feature in the adult model world was usually matched by the presence of the same feature in the child's form. However, the place of the feature in the child's form did not always correspond to the adult one; for example, a model word containing a final nasal might appear with nasality in the initial segment of the child's form. Waterson suggests that the child perceives utterances as whole units, and in perceiving the phonetic features of utterances may not necessarily be aware of their sequential ordering. This approach might explain some of the word forms in children's early speech that otherwise seem to lack an adult model. In this respect, Waterson's approach is complementary to that of investigators like Moscowitz (1970) and Menn (1971) who have concentrated on the syllabic and segmental properties of early words.

Waterson's assumptions about the child's perception, however, seem not to be borne out when carefully tested. Smith (1973) made careful tests of his child's perception of different adult forms not distinguished in the child's own productions. For example, his child used the form [maus] for both *mouth* and *mouse*. At the same time, the child made no errors when asked to pick out pictures of these objects. And the child appeared to have stored representations of the adult phonological forms such that the adult forms had priority. Consider the following dialogue (Smith, 1973, p. 137):

Adult: What does [maus] mean?
Child: Like a cat.
Adult: Yes: what else?
Child: Nothing else.
Adult: It's part of you.
Child: (disbelief)
Adult: It's part of your head.
Child: (fascinated)
Adult: (touching child's mouth) What's this?
Child: [maus]

Even then, the child took a few moments to realize that his production for *mouth* was the same as that for *mouse*. Smith (1973) argues these data (he reports a number of different examples) must result from the child's having set up the adult representations such that his own phonological rules are systematically related to the adult forms, rather than to a set of independent forms unique to the child along the lines suggested by Waterson. Smith shows on numerous occasions that the child first checks the adult representation (as in the above example) and only when that is rejected does he try to find some form based on his own phonetic form (cf. also Morton and Smith, 1974).

Lewis (1936) argued that the child masters the intonational patterns of his language before he begins to use sound sequences with any systematicity. However, the problem is one of deciding what mastery means. Lieberman (1967) pointed out that the infant cry is marked by a rising and then falling fundamental frequency contour, that falls most rapidly at the end just before the child breathes in again. He suggested therefore that the infant cry itself could be a precursor to the contours observed in the babbling stage (rise followed by fall) that are also typical of the declarative intonation patterns in many languages. Therefore, the use of such a fundamental frequency contour could be quite independent of any linguistic meaning that might be attached to it by an adult. Later on, however, the child has to learn more marked forms of contour; for example, contours with a final rise, where the child has to keep control of the airflow from his lungs (unlike the unmarked falling contour). Tonkova-Yampol'skaya (1969) compared the fundamental frequency and intensity characteristics of recordings from infants made during the first two years with adult intonation contours. She reported that the patterns of intonation matched the adult ones before there was any real match at the segmental level, but did not describe the data in any detail, nor did she give any information about the kinds of contexts in which children appeared to use different contours.

Since the observational studies in general do not provide very much contextual information about the one-word stage, it is unclear whether the child's earliest words are used only with one intonation pattern or with a range of different patterns to indicate different communicative functions, e.g., question versus request. If only a single intonation pattern occurs with each word, it could be the unmarked rise-fall described by Lieberman (1967) or it could consist of whatever contour it occurred with in the adult utterance from which the child picked up the word. Menyuk and Bernholtz (1969) carried out a preliminary study of one child in order to examine the hypothesis that all words occurred with the unmarked intonation contour. Repetitions of the same word from recordings of a child at the one-word stage were isolated and re-recorded. These words were from several adult word classes, and were all introduced by the child into the conversation, rather than being repetitions of adult utterances. Two listeners then tried to classify each isolated utterance as declarative, question or emphatic. Each word class contained examples of all three intonation types, except that proper names did not occur with emphatic contour. A spectrographic analysis revealed distinct characteristics for each intonation type, despite some variation within each category. Declaratives terminated with a falling contour, questions with a rising contour, and emphatics showed a sharp rise followed by a fall. These data suggest that intonation contours are probably used independently of the word even in the early stages, with some communicative intent. However, the early occurrence of intonation contours correlated with different communicative functions in the child's speech requires further investigation before it can be assumed that the child actually had the same communicative intent as the adult (cf. Halliday, 1973).

Perception and speech sounds
While the infant presumably pays attention to what goes on around him, and indeed gives evidence of being able to localize sound sources immediately after birth (Wertheimer, 1961), it is difficult to find out what it is that the child actually perceives. Even if the infant does discriminate differences between one sound and another, one does not know which parameter and which combination of parameters are necessary for the child to do this. Nor does the fact of discrimination alone tell us how the child goes from discrimination among speech sounds to recognition of their meaningfulness in speech. Research on adult speech perception has revealed a good deal about the cues used in the perception and discrimination of speech sounds. This research has also led to methods of generating synthetic speech materials in which the different parameters can be systematically varied for experimental purposes. This kind of variation is not feasible in the case of actual speech recordings being used as stimuli. The adult speech perception research has also led investigators to ask whether certain aspects of speech perception might not be innate for species-specific reasons (Morse, 1972). If this were the case, the infant might be expected to discriminate speech from nonspeech sounds fairly early on, and his ability to discriminate among speech sounds might also be expected to resemble adult discrimination.

Just as several stages have been noted in the kinds of sounds the infant produces during the course of the first year, so one can divide up the child's ability to perceive speech. However, since most of the studies report on observational data, more recent experimental work has tended to re-open a number of issues and to cast some doubt on the proposals put forward in the past. Kaplan and Kaplan (1970), in their review of the literature, described some five stages in perception of speech. These stages, however, are much less well delimited in perception than in production because of the paucity of reliable data and because of the few ages and few discriminations that have been systematically tested.

At the first stage, the infant is able to localize sounds, and within a few weeks appears to pay attention to differences in frequency, temporal patterning and duration of sounds (Spears and Hohle, 1967). Secondly, from about two weeks on, the infant appears able to discriminate the sound of voices from other sounds (bells, whistles and rattles). The evidence for this discrimination is from Wolff (1966) who found that voices were more effective in stopping an infant's crying. At the third stage, from about two months on, the infant responds differently to affective voice qualities. Angry voices are more likely to induce crying, while friendly ones elicit smiling and cooing. Wolff (1963) observed that infants at this stage also seemed to distinguish between familiar and unfamiliar voices, while Kaplan (1969) found that four-month-old infants could distinguish between female and male voices.

By the fourth stage, beginning at about five or six months, the infant appears to be sensitive to the intonational and rhythmic properties of adult speech. Lewis (1936), for example, argued that, of the two components of speech (segmental and intonational), the infant first learns to discriminate intonational patterns, and only later learns to discriminate segmental or phonetic differences. This position has been accepted by a large number of researchers. However, the studies that Lewis relied on were not necessarily a real test of the infant's discriminatory ability for intonational versus segmental factors (cf. Morse, 1972). Furthermore, several recent experimental studies (Eimas, Siqueland, Jusczyk, and Vigorito, 1971) have demonstrated that infants as young as one month can discriminate between two synthetic syllables that differ only in voicing, [ba] versus [pa]. These data could be used to propose the exact reverse of Lewis' position, particularly when combined with Kaplan's (1969) data on the perception of intonation. Using natural language recordings of the phrase *See the cat*, Kaplan found that eight-month olds could discriminate rising and falling intonation patterns combined with normal terminal stress. The issue, however, may rather be one of simple discrimination of differences, beginning from an early stage in life, compared to discrimination *with recognition* of consistently meaningful speech material.

One of the first studies of infant perception of differences between speech sounds was carried out by Moffitt (1968, 1971). He used a heart-rate measure with habituation to examine five-month olds' ability to discriminate the synthetic syllables [ba] and [ga]. The acoustic difference between the two syllables in real speech is one caused by the difference in place of articulation; [b] is a labial stop, made with closure of the lips, while [g] is a velar stop, made by closure between the back of the tongue and the roof of the mouth. Moffitt's results showed that infants aged five months could discriminate this difference. Eimas *et al.* (1970), using rate of non-nutritive sucking as their measure, looked at the discrimination of voicing in the syllable pair [pa] versus [ba] in infants aged one month and four months. They found that both age groups could make this discrimination.

Morse (1972) looked at three different factors in the ability of seven-week old infants to discriminate. He tested place of articulation, with the synthetic syllables [ba] and [ga], and intonation pattern, with the unmarked fall [ba−] and the more marked rise contour [ba+] superimposed on the syllable. Thirdly, he isolated acoustic cues from the onset portions of the two syllables, [ba] and [ga], to produce two chirp-like, non-speech sounds. The data showed that the place of articulation group managed to discriminate the difference between [ba] and [ga], thus replicating Moffitt's results on a much younger age group (seven weeks rather than five months). The data also showed that infants this age discriminated between the two intonation contours, [ba−] versus [ba+]. However, the group presented with the non-speech condition, the chirp-like sounds derived from acoustic cues from [ba] and [ga], failed to discriminate when a change occurred in the stimulus. This result is compatible with the hypothesis mentioned earlier—that infants might be expected to show some similarity to adults in their perception of speech sounds—because, like adults, they did notice the change in the speech sound, but failed to notice the change in the non-speech sound. One might therefore conclude that infants are not just noticing differences, but rather are selecting particular acoustic cues characteristic of speech alone when they make such discriminations. Eimas (1975) also reports on a replication of the Eimas *et al.* (1971) results with another syllable pair, [da] versus [ta].

While these results add to the generality of the findings thus far, the nature of the mechanisms that allow the young infant to discriminate among different speech sounds and the relation of this ability to later language development needs much further exploration (cf. Morse, 1974). What is clear at this point is that there may be a difference between the infant's ability to make some discrimination and the point in time at which the infant realizes that such a discrimination may play a particular role in a communicative system.

The fifth stage posited by Kaplan and Kaplan (1970) is marked by the infant's ability to distinguish some of the segmental oppositions that play a role in the phonological structure of the language. This stage in speech perception coincides with the child's first productions of such oppositions, towards the end of the first year (Jakobson, 1941/1968). Most studies have concentrated on the child's ability to produce particular forms, though, and the question of what the child perceives to be phonemic oppositions has only been investigated in a couple of studies.

Shvachkin (1948/1973) was concerned with the role played by articulation and by hearing in the acquisition of phonemic distinctions. He argued that perception and articulatory ability were not sufficient to account for phonemic development, and that, in fact, the guiding factor was semantics. It is only when the child realizes that a *different meaning* is at issue that he will learn systematic oppositions among the sounds of his language. In order to investigate the development of such systematic discriminations, Shvachkin used the technique of teaching very young children (10 months to 2;0 years) the names of geometric shapes and certain everyday objects. The names were nonsense syllables of the form VC or CVC. Having determined in pilot work that the initial position in a word seemed more salient, Shvachkin used syllables in which initial vowels contrasted, as in /ak/ and /ik/, in which the initial consonant was in contrast with zero, as in /ak/ and /bak/, and in which the initial consonants contrasted, as in /mak-bak/, /bak-dak/, /bak-pak/, etc. The child's discrimination of these phonemic contrasts was tested by asking him to pick out the toy named /mak/, say, in a context where he had the toys /mak/ and /bak/ present. Unless he had learnt that sonorants (/m/) contrasted with stops (/b/), the child would fail to pick the right object over a series of trials, even though he was quite able to pick out /bak/ or /mak/ separately when they were presented beside a toy named /zub/.

Shvachkin found a distinct order of acquisition in the perception of these different phonemic contrasts which he described as twelve stages, and, on the whole, his ordering for perception is remarkably close to the ordering noted by Jakobson (1941/1968) for production. The ordering of the twelve stages is remarkably consistent across the nine children tested for all twelve over a period of six to eight months, with a high average rank correlation for order among the children, $r \cong \cdot 97$. A further six children were tested on the first seven stages, and showed equally strong agreement, $r = \cdot 94$. Thus, the data contributed by Shvachkin make a strong argument in favour of a consistent order of acquisition in the discrimination of various classes of phonemic contrasts.

There are, however, a few points in Shvachkin's study that have provoked queries. His methodology is clearly described, but has proved rather hard to replicate in exactly the form reported (cf. Garnica, 1973). Secondly, he gave no account of the number of trials over which each child was actually tested for each contrast, nor did he make explicit the criterion used in attributing such knowledge to the child. (His article does suggest, though, that the criterion was 'all instances correct', cf. Shvachkin, 1973, p. 102.) Garnica (1973) discussed these problems in presenting a preliminary account of a study designed to test Shvachkin's proposal that the order of acquisition was universal, varying only in terms of the classes of oppositions that actually play a role in the language being learnt. For example, the opposition between palatalised and non-palatalised consonants is not phonemic in English, so one should not expect to see such a stage in English-speaking children. The ordering of oppositions for English appears to show somewhat more variability across children than Shvachkin reported. More detailed analyses will be required, though, before it will be possible to draw any firm conclusions about the ontogenetic universality of the order in which children learn to perceive phonemic oppositions.

McCarthy (1954) reported on a large number of studies that looked at the sounds children of different ages could generally pronounce in an adult fashion. However, there has been little or no work on older children's perception of sounds. The fact that pronunciation does not necessarily mirror perception is shown by the many reported instances of what has come to be called 'the *fis* phenomenon'. Children presented with imitations of their own productions, e.g., *fis* for *fish*, reject the imitated form, and will only accept the adult *fish*, even though, in their own speech, they do not distinguish *s* from *sh* (Berko and Brown, 1960; Smith and Morton, 1974).

One other area of phonological development that has been explored is the child's knowledge of the sequence rules that govern the possible combinations of sounds. These rules specify the possible (but not necessarily occurring) sequences for a language. For example, monolingual speakers of English recognize that Lewis Carroll's *slithy toves* constitute possible English words. At the same time, they would reject *mbaq* or *dvorn*. Messer (1967) examined the choices made by three-and-a-half year olds of potential names for toys from among words that conformed and words that did not conform to the rules of sequence for English. His results showed that the monolingual children chose possible English sequences significantly more often than they chose impossible sequences. Furthermore, they mispronounced the impossible forms more often, changing them minimally so as to be closer to possible English forms. An analysis of three children who had been exposed to a second language, and who appeared to have chosen possible English forms at a chance level, showed that they too demonstrated knowledge of possible sequences for English *and* their second language combined. Messer concluded that by this age, children have internalized the rules of combination for the sounds of their language. This not only predisposes them to pick out possible English sequences, but also leads them to mispronounce impossible sequences. Further investigation might reveal when such integration of phonological knowledge takes place, and how soon the child starts to observe such rules in his own speech (e.g., Menn, 1971). It is possible that the child would not have the full set of rules until he had learnt all the possible positions for different sounds, occurring both singly and in clusters.

LANGUAGE INPUT TO CHILDREN

A moment's reflection will tell the speaker of English (or of any other language) that he does not speak in exactly the same way to everyone he addresses. While his speech style may vary with mood (good or bad temper) or physical condition (tired or ill versus wide awake), he also varies it independently of such factors. For example, he will speak more formally to those he does not know well, or has only just met, than he will to members of his own family or to colleagues he sees every day. The choice of speech style is determined by a complex set of social conditions that hold in particular situations (e.g., the differences between attending a party, joining a work-crew, being a pupil versus a teacher in a classroom, being a hospital patient, and so on). The situation itself is probably one of the main factors in deciding on the appropriate degree of formality or informality to use. Other contributing factors probably include relative social status (either hereditary or conferred by the situation), employment, income, and so on (cf. Ervin-Tripp, 1973).

Many languages make the choice of a formal speech style explicit in the actual utterance by adding different particles, using particular address terms or particular pronoun forms in addition to use of slower, more carefully pronounced speech. Informal speech may also be marked by use of special pronoun forms (cf. Brown and

Gilman, 1960) and, in English at least, tends to be more rapid, with more unstressed syllables, more contracted forms, and so on. These differences in speech style among adults talking to each other have received relatively little notice from investigators of language acquisition.

The first part of this section will detail some of the findings from both observational and experimental studies of how adults speak to children, and how their speech to children differs markedly from their speech to other adults. The second part of this section will deal with some of the modifications that are made and their potential utility to the child learning language. The possible importance of the input data on language has been generally overlooked until recently. In part, this neglect followed from the virtual dismissal of speech performance as relevant to linguistic theory (e.g., Chomsky, 1965), and in part from the emphasis on innate mechanisms as an explanation for how, and how quickly, the child acquires his first language (e.g., McNeill, 1966). The recent push to integrate the study of language with cognition and cognitive development in general has forced some re-examination of this issue, and has induced investigators to take a closer look at the kind of input that the child is expected to process at different stages in his linguistic development.

Speech addressed to children
The speech used by adults to other adults has frequently been described as being full of false starts, hesitations, slips of the tongue, and being generally made up of ungrammatical utterances (e.g., Chomsky, 1967; Bever, Fodor and Weksel, 1965). Moreover, since adult speech was seen as usually ungrammatical, it was assumed that the language input to children was also ungrammatical, and was therefore of minimal import for the child acquiring language. This hardly mattered, though, given there were innate mechanisms for the acquisition of language, which really did not need the language input except possibly to trigger these mechanisms.

Other linguists have vigorously contested the view that everyday adult speech is largely ungrammatical. Labov (1970), for example, pointed out that:

The ungrammaticality of everyday speech seems to be a myth with no basis in actual fact. In the various empirical studies that we have conducted, the great majority of utterances—about 75 per cent—are well formed by any criterion. When rules of ellipsis are applied, and certain universal editing rules to take care of stammering and false starts, the proportion of truly ungrammatical and ill-formed sentences falls to less than two per cent. (1970, p. 42)

Furthermore, several investigators of children's language early noted that the speech of adults to children did differ from their speech to other adults. For example, Brown and Bellugi (1964) observed that 'The mother's speech differs from the speech that adults use to one another in many ways. Her sentences are short and simple; . . . Perhaps because they are short, the sentences of the mother are perfectly grammatical' (1964, p. 135). More recently, Waterson (1971) noticed that both grammatical and phonological deviance seemed very rare in the speech addressed directly to children (cf. also Halliday, 1975).

More systematic investigation into the kind of speech used by adults to children has shown that adults indeed use much simpler sentences, with few or no embedded or conjoined clauses, use different proportions of certain sentence-types, speak more slowly to younger children, use a different pattern of pausing to younger children, use a much more restricted vocabulary, produce very few mistakes and hardly any ungrammatical sentences (Farwell, 1973).

Sachs, Brown and Salerno (1972) found that adults (who had no children of their own) used simpler sentence structure when telling a story to a child aged 1;10 than when telling it to another adult. Similar findings are reported by Snow (1972a) and Phillips (1973). The number of sentences used in a set period of time was significantly greater for continuous speech to the child, mainly because the sentences used were much shorter (Sachs et al., 1972). Snow (1972a) also found that adults used shorter sentences when speaking to a two-year old than when talking to a ten-year old. These shorter sentences contained fewer inflexions than utterances addressed to ten-year olds or adults. Adults use a significantly greater number of complex sentences (relative clauses, complements, subordinate clauses) in addressing adults than in addressing children (Sachs et al., 1972; Drach, 1968).

When rate of speech was considered, Sachs et al. (1972) found that adults used significantly more words per minute to other adults than to children. Broen (1972) reported that adults spoke twice as fast to each other as to children, and also that the rate of speech to children varied significantly with age of child. Thus, adults spoke more slowly to children between 1;6 and 2;2 than to children between 4;0 and 6;0 years. Broen (1972) also observed that in addressing children, particularly younger ones, adults paused almost exclusively at sentence boundaries. Furthermore, almost all the utterances addressed to the younger group (1;6-2;2) were followed by a pause. In speech to adults, the pauses seemed to be distributed half and half between inter-sentential and intra-sentential positions. The pattern of pauses in speech to children aged 4;0-6;0 looked more like the speech to younger children, but it did contain some within-sentence pauses. The placement of pauses, then, would seem to be another factor, in addition to rate of speech, that varies with the age of the addressee.

Broen found that there were significant differences in the type-token ratio for the speech of adult-to-adult and the speech of adult-to-child, where the children were aged between 4;0 and 6;0. There were also significant differences in the type-token ratios for adult speech to the older versus younger children, such that the number of different words used to the younger children was very restricted. Phillips (1973) also found significant differences in the vocabulary range used to adults versus that used to children under 2;4. Many fewer different words were used when the parents were speaking to young children.

The sentence-types used in speech to children seem to be fairly evenly divided among simple declaratives, questions and imperatives. Blount (1972) reported about two-thirds of the input utterances were interrogatives, while the other third was equally divided among declarative and imperative forms. This contrasted with adult-to-adult speech where the majority of the utterances (70%) were declaratives. Drach (1968) found that about one third of the utterances addressed to the child were imperatives (34 out of 111); questions were also very frequent and accounted for 50% of the input forms. On the other hand, negatives were very rare, compared to their rate of occurrence in adult-to-adult speech. Lastly, Drach (1968) found that there were ten times as many subordinate clauses in the utterances addressed to other adults. The relative proportion of questions addressed to the child was close to that reported by Blount. Sachs *et al.* (1972) also found that adults used significantly more question forms (i.e., with final rising intonation) when telling a story to a very young child than when telling it to an adult. Sachs suggests that such question forms may not really be questions; instead the rising intonation pattern may simply be used to catch the child's attention, or else to signal a sentential boundary. Ervin-Tripp (1970) suggested that the high proportion of interrogative forms reflects the adult's attempts to get feedback about whether the child has understood or not. Broen (1972) found that the speech addressed to children was fairly evenly divided among interrogatives (mainly yes/no), imperatives, and simple declaratives, with about 30% of each in her samples. The remaining 10% of input utterances consisted of single words. Pfuderer (1968) found roughly similar proportions of simple sentence types in the speech addressed to three young children. She then looked at the changes in complexity among the input utterances at two later stages in these children's development and found that the complexity of adult speech increased as the children acquired more language. However, it was not clear whether there was any direct relationship between the form of the increase in adult complexity and the child's growing linguistic knowledge.

Ferguson *et al.* (1973) observed that new items of vocabulary seemed to be introduced through use in set sentence frames such as *Where's————, Here comes————, Look at————, There's————,* and *Listen to————.* Broen (1972) also found that parents use such frames very frequently, with as many as five instances of the same frame within a five-minute period. This type of frame was common in all the mothers' speech. Both Broen (1972) and Snow (1972a) found that few third-person pronouns were used in addressing young children. Instead the adult repeats the whole noun phrase in the following sentence. The incidence of repetitions generally was also high (cf. also Kobashigawa, 1968). Snow (1972a) found that many of the utterances addressed to young children consisted of repetitions of simple noun phrases, prepositional phrases and a few verbless (copular) sentences, generally repeated immediately after the full sentence form. She also found that some 14% of the utterances to two-year olds consisted of paraphrases, e.g., *'Give mummy all the red toys. I would like all the things that look like this. Can you give me all the red things?'* This occurred three times as frequently as for the ten-year-olds. The repetitions seem designed to draw the child's attention to particular parts of the utterance, while many of the paraphrases seemed to be elicited by the child's not attending to the first utterance. Non-attention was often construed as non-comprehension.

Shipley, Smith and Gleitman (1969) got mothers to catch their children's attention and then give them commands of the following sort:

Throw me the ball!	Throw ronta ball!
Throw ball!	Gor me the ball!
Please, Johnnie, throw ball!	Gor ronta ball!
Ball!	Gor ball!

As long as the child either looked at the object named, pointed to it, or gave some verbal response, he was judged to have answered the command in a relevant fashion. The younger children in this experiment, at the one-word stage, responded best to commands that were telegraphic (*Throw ball!*) or contained only one word. Slightly older children, in the two-word stage, gave evidence of responding more readily to the full adult forms than to the telegraphic forms that were closest to their own speech. These children also did better on the actual utterances than they did on those containing nonsense words, except for the command which had the nonsense word embedded between two real words (*Throw ronta ball!*) which was treated as quite normal. Thus the older children responded better to the more complex linguistic form used as a command. Snow (1972b) reported similar findings for a preliminary study modelled on Shipley *et al.* (1969) that she plans to carry out longitudinally. Her test sentences cover a greater variety of forms: questions, commands and suggestions, all demanding a response within the child's abilities. She plans to compare the forms that do elicit responses in any one test session with those that fail to elicit responses, and also to make the same comparisons across time by re-testing children at two monthly intervals. Such comparisons should allow one to order the input sentences according to some measure of complexity. Such an ordering should also assist in the identification of the features of speech that the child attends to at different stages.

Smith (1970) suggested that the young child responds only to familiar words occurring in sentence initial position; hence the lack of response in the Shipley *et al.* study to commands beginning with a nonsense word. Other observers have noticed that the language that seems to be most important for the child himself is language addressed directly to the child. This would explain why the very young child often ignores language from the radio or television. Shipley *et al.* (1969) also found that young children would not respond to the tape-recorded voices that they used first for giving the test commands. The young child's selective attention to what he understands at different stages of development could also be one of the controlling factors in parents' choice of simpler sentence forms. The parents have learnt, from experience, that more complex forms do not produce any response from the child. Similarly, the abundant use of paraphrase by many parents speaking to two-year olds may simply be a way of making sure that the child will understand from one or other of the forms given what is required of him. The other modifications that are used in speaking to the young child (that may also play a role in catching and holding his attention) are prosodic ones, e.g., raised pitch, occasional vowel lengthening, whispering, exaggerated intonation and stress patterns, and greater overall variation in the intonation contour (cf. Garnica, 1975).

Lastly, the regular and pervasive nature of the modifications made in adult speech when addressing children is further attested by the fact that children by about the age of 8;0 or 9;0 have learnt many of the same modifications and use them in speaking to younger siblings and other younger children (Berko Gleason, 1973). Gelman and Shatz (1972) found that even children as young as four years of age modified their speech when talking to two-year olds. Moreover, they simplified more in the case of children who were just 2;0 than in the case of those who were nearly 3;0. Simplifications consisted of omitting verbs, use of repetitions, frequent use of the younger child's name or other attention-getting words such as *Look, Here,* etc. They also used many more one-word utterances and many fewer compound and complex sentences than they did to peers or to adults (cf. also Shatz and Gelman, 1973). Andersen and Johnson (1973) studied the modifications made by one eight-year old to children of varying ages. They used a number of measures that have been reported elsewhere, and found that the eight-year old systematically modified her speech so that she used the shortest, syntactically simplest, forms with the youngest child, with a gradual increase of complexity with older and older children. Peers and adults were not differentiated.

Aids to language acquisition?

Adults undoubtedly do use a different style of speech when they talk to young children. They use simpler sentences, and appear to provide a number of prosodic clues to indicate sentence boundaries; their use of repetitions may also provide information about sentence constituent boundaries. The main questions that these observations raise are the following: (1) do such modifications have any beneficial effect on the child who is in the process of acquiring language, and (2) are such modifications a necessary condition for the acquisition of a first language?

In discussing the strategies and operating principles that children bring to language-learning, investigators such as Slobin (1973) and Bever (1970a) have concentrated heavily on problems of segmentation, the identification by the child of sentence boundaries, constituent boundaries, and the isolation of the inflexional markers for different grammatical roles. Several of the modifications made by parents in their speech seem to be designed specifically to provide the child with information about such boundaries. First of all, parents use a number of different sentence frames for new words, e.g.

$$
\left\{
\begin{array}{l}
\text{Where's} \\
\text{Let's play with} \\
\text{Look at} \\
\text{See} \\
\text{Listen to} \\
\text{Here's} \\
\text{Here comes}
\end{array}
\right\}
\ \text{---}\
\left\{
\begin{array}{l}
\text{Mummy} \\
\text{Daddy} \\
\text{(the) doggie} \\
\text{---} \\
\text{---}
\end{array}
\right\}
$$

These frames often carry an exaggerated intonation contour, with heavy stress on the final word (Farwell, 1973; Ferguson *et al.*, 1973; Broen, 1972). While such frames clearly provide the child with certain information about the segmentation of the final word, they may also be responsible for the incorrect segmentation of part of the frame, e.g., *thats* with no realization that the /-s/ is part of the copula verb, or *itsa* (cf. Brown, 1973).

Another clue to segmentation in the earliest stages might be the pattern of pauses used by the adult. When talking to very young children (1;6 or so), adults tend to pause only at the ends of sentences; moreover, they do this at the end of nearly every sentence (Broen, 1972). Intonation contours probably also play a role in marking sentential boundaries. Sachs *et al.* (1972) observed that adults reading to a two-year old used a large number of question-intonation contours (final rise), and conjectured that this may be a boundary marker and a way of holding the child's attention. The test for its use as a boundary marker would have to come from a language that did not use rising intonation to mark yes/no questions.

Another aid to segmentation of the input language by the child might be the repetitions provided by the adult. Snow (1972a) found that up to 8% of the utterances addressed to two-year olds were repeated by the parent shortly afterwards. In repeating a constituent, the mothers often placed it in a new sentence frame at the same time, e.g., *'Pick up the red one. Find the red one. Not the green one. I want the red one. Can you find the red one?'* This would provide the child with two kinds of information: segmental information about the constituent boundaries, and structural information about the kinds of frames with which such a constituent may be used. This repetition of a constituent in different frames might also be one source of the practice sequences reported by Weir (1962). As Snow pointed out, these repetitions would also give the child more processing time for trying to interpret the sentence, because they provide prompts as to the constituent structure and thus save the child from having to remember the whole sentence at once. Another aid that is closely related to this use of repetition by the adult is that provided by paraphrases involving lexical substitutions, changes in word order and, of course, the use of different sentence frames that are related in meaning. Bowerman (1973a) reported that the mothers of the Finnish children in her study frequently repeated utterances to the child but changed the word order. This again would give the child additional information about the boundaries between constituents. Paraphrase, and the concomitant use of lexical substitution for various constituents, would provide the child with information both about segmentation and about relatedness among lexical items.

The adult appears to adjust the complexity of his utterances to the age of the listener. The younger the child, the simpler the syntactic forms that are used in speaking to him. At the same time, the data from Shipley *et al.* (1969) suggest that children attend to utterances that are at the next stage up in complexity from their own productions. Children at the one-word stage responded best to single-word commands and to telegraphic commands, e.g., *Ball!* and *Throw ball!* The children at the two-word stage, however, responded best to the full adult form of command, e.g., *Throw the ball!* If this kind of pacing, where the adult input is always one level or so above the child's own productions, is used consistently by adults speaking to children, it would provide an excellent model to the child of what the next stage should be, as far as his own developing structures were concerned. Although this hypothesis would need careful testing, Pfuderer's (1968) observations suggest that the increase in complexity in the adult input may not necessarily be directly geared to the child's next stage of development. However, Blount (1972) did find that the kinds of questions asked to young children were closely tied to their level of comprehension. In order for adults to be able to set their speech at an appropriate level of complexity for the child, it is clear that there has to be feedback from the child himself. This may be one reason for the high percentage of questions present in the language input to young children. Since the child's language develops relatively rapidly, the adult has continually to readjust his own speech, based on his estimates of how much the child can understand at each stage. The adjustments, therefore, may be forced on the adult by the child himself, provided the adult wishes to communicate. The extent to which the adult's adjustments actually foreshadow the next stage in the child's language development, however, remains to be investigated.

Several researchers have referred to certain types of adult input explicitly as 'training situations'. Brown, Cazden and Bellugi (1969) suggested that certain types of dialogue may involve language coaching. For example, if the child produces a telegraphic utterance, the adult may *expand* it, by repeating it back to the child with the adult inflexions and function words filled in:

Child: Baby chair.
Adult: Yes, the baby's sitting in the chair.

Instead of expanding the child's utterance, the adult may instead *model* it. Modelling involves carrying on the conversation, and simply adding to what the child has said by providing additional information about the topic, e.g.:

Child: Baby chair.
Adult: Do you want to sit at the table too?

Modelling often involves some paraphrase as well, and may involve repetition of the lexical items originally used by the child. A third situation that Brown *et al.* (1969) describe is one in which the parent *echoes* the child, as in:

Child: I saw the XXX.
Adult: You saw the what?

This use of echoing, of course, is yet another way of segmenting the sentence constituents, apart from telling the child that he has not made himself understood. Brown *et al.*'s fourth teaching situation is *prompting*. They suggested that this situation helps to demonstrate preposing of Wh question words, and to show what constituents they substitute for:

Adult: What did you see?
Child: [no answer]
Adult: You saw *what*?

They found that the second question form, *You saw what?*, was often better for eliciting some answer from the child. Ervin-Tripp (1970) suggested a fifth training situation, where the adult models a question *and* an appropriate response sequence, as in:

Adult: Where's the ball? Here's the ball.

Such sequences usually carry exaggerated intonation contours. This explicit demonstration of the appropriate answers to different question types also provides the child with examples of dialogue (cf. Halliday, 1975).

Cazden (1965) carried out one of the only studies that has attempted to test the value to the child of deliberately expanding his utterances. She looked at the effects of expansion and modelling versus a non-treatment control group for a set of two-year-old children attending a day-care centre. One group received 40 minutes of expansion training daily during which the experimenter systematically expanded every utterance produced by the child. The second group received 40 minutes of modelling daily, where the adult simply expatiated upon whatever the child had said, but refrained from repeating the lexical items used by the child. At the end of twelve weeks, the two groups and the control group retook a set of language tests that had been administered at the beginning of the study. The results showed that, contrary to Cazden's initial hypothesis, the expansion and control groups showed little difference. The modelling group, however, had progressed significantly further than either the expansion group or the control. Cazden concluded that exposure to more language for talking about the world around the child was therefore more important from the input point of view than just expansion of the child's own utterances. One difficulty with the study is that the situation in which an adult expands or models only in a particular way is probably not a natural one. Most children are exposed to some of each. Therefore the degree to which either expansion or modelling may affect the child's language development requires further investigation (cf. McNeill, 1970).

It is evident that parental speech may provide the child with a good deal of the information about how to segment sentence constitutions and about permissible combinations of such constituents. These data, therefore, do provide a tentative answer to the first question that was posed about parental input. The modifications in adult speech presumably serve to inform the child about the structure of the language he is learning. The kind of information given in this way seems highly pertinent to the sorts of strategy that the child seems to adopt in the early stages for both interpretation and production of language (cf. Slobin, 1973). However, the fact remains that we are no nearer to finding an answer to the second question that was put: are such modifications in input a necessary condition for the acquisition of language by the child?

This question is of critical importance from the theoretical point of view. The answer to it will be very important to any theory of language acquisition. In fact, because of the emphasis on innate mechanisms of some (unspecified) nature, investigators such as Fodor have claimed that 'it would be methodologically sound to assume that the child's increasing linguistic proficiency is not to be attributed to any significant extent to the special character of the utterances he hears' (1966, p. 108). This approach, though, may turn out not to be so sound after all in the light of the extensive modifications that adults do make in their speech to children. The fact that children also appear to screen out anything in the way of linguistic input that they do not understand argues against Fodor's (1966) point that much of the linguistic input to the child is actually 'overheard speech' from adult to adult. The most important thing may simply be for adults to speak to children and to encourage them to talk back. It is possible, of course, that adult input to the child acts mainly as a trigger to set off the particular mechanisms that deal with speech processing. However, learning language is not just a matter of learning particular linguistic structures, it is also a matter of learning how to use them in order to communicate. If the parent finds he has to modify his speech to the child in order to achieve this, the child will receive these modifications as input. Furthermore, it is extremely hard to assess the exact effect of training situations such as those noted by Brown *et al.* (1969). All in all, while the modifications made by adults might not be *necessary* conditions for the child's acquisition of linguistic structure, it is possible that they may play a crucial role in his learning *how* to use language in order to communicate with others.

In this chapter, I have singled out those areas of research on language acquisition that, in conjunction with one another, raise many of the questions that will be central to a theory of first language acquisition. Particularly important is the renewed interest in the relation between language and cognitive development, and the observation that the child's linguistic development seems to be paced by his cognitive development (Slobin, 1973). Furthermore, the kinds of strategies and operating principles that the child brings to the task of acquiring a first language also seem to be an outgrowth of his general cognitive development (Bever, 1970a, 1970b; Slobin, 1973; Clark, 1973c, 1974).

Another side of language development that has attracted relatively little attention is the child's knowledge of what to say when, his social uses of language to communicate appropriately in different social settings (Ervin-Tripp, 1971, 1973). While it is clear that even the four-year old has already acquired some skill in this domain and, for example, systematically modifies his speech in talking to younger children (Shatz and Gelman, 1973), the range of modifications possible and the rules governing their usage in different situations are immensely complex (cf. Ervin-Tripp, 1973; Labov, 1970). Berko Gleason's (1973) observations suggest that the eight- or nine-year old has a number of different styles at his command, and a considerable knowledge of the appropriate contexts in which to use them. In addition to learning what style of speech to use under various circumstances, the child also has to learn how to take part in a conversation, how to enter a conversation, what constitutes an appropriate answer to a question or request, and so on (Grice, 1967). Many of these conventions have a more general role: they are the conventions for behaviour within a particular group or society. Thus, in learning language, the child is also learning how to behave (Berko Gleason, 1973).

The acquisition of semantics, and in particular of lexical meaning, has only recently been taken up (Clark, 1973b). The study of what the child actually means, as opposed to what the adult would mean using the same words, opens the question of the extent to which any of the child's early utterances can be analysed from an adult standpoint. Some of the data on children's earliest word meanings suggest that an adult-based analysis of, say, the child's verbs may attribute more to the child than he actually knows (cf. Schlesinger, 1974). The study of early word meanings and the kind of information the child encodes also raises the question of the exact relationship between the child's cognitive system and the semantics of the language he is learning. Meaning and the interpretation of any sort of input have to be able to map onto one another so that one can communicate. The nature of this mapping remains to be further explored in both adult and child.

Lastly, there is one area of research, not mentioned in this chapter, that promises to tell us more about what the child himself knows about language as a system. Adults can usually make a variety of meta-linguistic judgements about what they say and hear. While such skills may be the stock-in-trade of the linguist, they are clearly not confined to linguists. Gleitman, Gleitman and Shipley (1972) have begun to explore the child's capacity to make meta-linguistic statements about the language that he uses. They began from the observation that even quite young children often ask why some form is the way it is, e.g.:

Child: Mommy, is it AN A-dult or A NUH-dult?

and gave children between the ages of 5;0 and 8;0 a number of deviant sentences about which to make judgements. Not only did the children have to say whether the sentences were all right or not, but they were also asked to explain why the sentences seemed wrong. In the course of making such judgements, most of the children also supplied appropriate forms, together with surprisingly sophisticated explanations. This research provides yet another avenue of approach to the problem of finding out what the child actually knows. The soliciting of such judgements differs from the simple collection of spontaneous speech because the child has to justify his meta-linguistic decisions. The integration of such judgmental data with other studies of language acquisition should hasten the time when an adequate theory of acquisition can be put forward.

Amidon, A. and Carey, P. (1972). Why five-year olds cannot understand *before* and *after*. *Journal of Verbal Learning and Verbal Behavior*, **11**, 417-23.

Andersen, E. and Johnson, C. (1973). Modifications in the speech of an eight-year old to younger children. *Stanford Occasional Papers in Linguistics*, Stanford University, **3**, 149-60.

Anisfeld, M. and Tucker, G. R. (1968). English pluralization rules of six-year old children. *Children Development*, **38**, 1201-17.

Antinucci, F. and Parisi, D. (1973). Early language acquisition: a model and some data. In Ferguson, C. A. and Slobin, D. I. (Eds.), *Studies of child language development*. New York: Holt, Rinehart and Winston.

Austin, J. L. (1962). *How to do things with words*. Oxford: Oxford University Press.

Bellugi, U. (1971). Simplification in children's language. In Huxley, R. and Ingram E., (Eds.) *Methods and models in language acquisition*. New York: Academic Press.

Bellugi, U. and Brown, R. (Eds.) (1964). *The acquisition of language. Monographs of the Society for Research in Child Development*, **29**.

Bendix, E. H. (1966). *Componential analysis of general vocabulary: the semantic structure of a set of verbs in English, Hindi and Japanese*. The Hague: Mouton.

Berko, J. (1958). The child's learning of English morphology. *Word*, **14**, 150-77.

Berko Gleason, J. (1973). Code switching in children's language. In Moore, T. E. (Ed.), *Cognitive development and the acquisition of language*. New York: Academic Press.

Berko, J. and Brown, R. (1960). Psycholinguistic research methods. In Mussen, P. H. (Ed.), *Handbook of research methods in child development*. New York: Wiley.

Bever, T. G. (1970a). The cognitive basis for linguistic structures. In Hayes, J. R. (Ed.), *Cognition and the development of language*. New York: Wiley.

Bever, T. G. (1970b). The integrated study of language behavior. In Morton, J. (Ed.), *Biological and social factors in psycholinguistics*. Urbana, Ill.: University of Illinois Press.

Bever, T. G., Fodor, J. A. and Weksel, W. (1965). Theoretical notes on the acquisition of syntax: critique of 'contextual generalization'. *Psychological Review*, **72**, 467-82.

Bierwisch, M. (1967). Some universals of German adjectivals. *Foundations of Language*, **3**, 1-36.

Bierwisch, M. (1969). On certain problems of semantic representations. *Foundations of Language*, **5**, 153-84.

Bierwisch, M. (1970). Semantics. In Lyons, J. (Ed.), *New horizons in linguistics*. Harmondsworth: Penguin Books.

Bloom, L. M. (1970). *Language development: form and function in emerging grammars*. Cambridge, Mass.: MIT Press.

Bloom, L. M. (1971). Why not pivot grammar? *Journal of Speech and Hearing Disorders*, **36**, 40-50.

Bloom, L. M. (1973). *One word at a time: the use of single word utterances before syntax*. The Hague: Mouton.

Blount, B. G. (1972). Parental speech and language acquisition: some Luo and Samoan examples. *Anthropological Linguistics*, **14**, 119-30.

Blumenthal, A. L. (1970). *Language and psychology: historical aspects of psycholinguistics*. New York: Wiley.

Bogoyavlenskiy, D. N. (1957/1973). *Psikhologiya usvoyeniya orfografii*. Moscow: Akad. Pedag. Nauk RSFSR. Translated in Ferguson, C. A. and Slobin, D. I. (Eds.), *Studies of child language development*. New York: Holt, Rinehart and Winston.

Bolinger, D. L. (1965). The atomization of meaning. *Language*, **41**, 555-73.

Bowerman, M. F. (1973a). *Early syntactic development: a cross-linguistic study with special reference to Finnish*. Cambridge: Cambridge University Press.

Bowerman, M. F. (1973b). Structural relationships in children's utterances: syntactic or semantic? In Moore, T. E. (Ed.), *Cognitive development and the acquisition of language*. New York: Academic Press.

Braine, M. D. S. (1963). The ontogeny of English phrase structure: the first phrase. *Language*, **39**, 1-13.

Braine, M. D. S. (1971). The acquisition of language in infant and child. In Reed, C. E. (Ed.), *The learning of language*. New York: Appleton-Century-Crofts.

Broen, P. (1972). *The verbal environment of the language-learning child*. Monographs of the American Speech and Hearing Association, **17**.

Brown, H. D. (1971). Children's comprehension of relativized English sentences. *Child Development*, **42**, 1923-36.

Brown, R. (1968). The development of Wh questions in child speech. *Journal of Verbal Learning and Verbal Behavior*, **7**, 277-90.

Brown, R. (1973). *A first language: the early stages*. Cambridge, Mass.: Harvard University Press.

Brown, R. and Bellugi, U. (1964). Three processes in the acquisition of syntax. *Harvard Educational Review*, **34**, 133-51.

Brown, R., Cazden, C. B. and Bellugi, U. (1969). The child's grammar from I to III. In Hill, J. P. (Ed.), *Minnesota symposium on child psychology*, vol. 2. Minneapolis, Minn.: University of Minnesota Press.

Brown, R. and Gilman, A. (1960). The pronouns of power and solidarity. In Sebeok, T. A. (Ed.), *Style in language*. Cambridge, Mass.: MIT Press.

Brown, R. and Hanlon, C. (1970). Derivational complexity and order of acquisition in child speech. In Hayes, J. R. (Ed.), *Cognition and the development of language*. New York: Wiley.

Carter, A. (1973). Development of the pre-syntactic communication system: a case study. Paper presented at Society for Research in Child Development Meeting, Philadelphia.

Cazden, C. B. (1965). Environmental assistance to the child's acquisition of grammar. Unpublished Ph.D. thesis, Harvard University.

Chomsky, C. S. (1969). *The acquisition of syntax in children from 5 to 10*. Cambridge, Mass.: MIT Press.

Chomsky, N. (1957). *Syntactic structures*. The Hague: Mouton.

Chomsky, N. (1959). Review of Skinner, B. F.: *Verbal behavior. Language*, **35**, 26-58.

Chomsky, N. (1965). *Aspects of the theory of syntax*. Cambridge, Mass.: MIT Press.

Chomsky, N. (1967). The formal nature of language. Appendix A to Lenneberg, E. H., *Biological foundations of language*. New York: Wiley.

Chomsky, N. (1968). *Language and mind*. New York: Harcourt, Brace and World.

Clark, E. V. (1970). How young children describe events in time. In Flores d'Arcais, G. B. and Levelt, W. J. M. (Eds.), *Advances in psycholinguistics*. Amsterdam: North-Holland Publishing Co.

Clark, E. V. (1971a). On the acquisition of the meaning of *before* and *after*. *Journal of Verbal Learning and Verbal Behavior*, **10**, 266-75.

Clark, E. V. (1971b). Review of Chomsky, C. S. *The acquisition of syntax in children from 5 to 10. Language*, **47**, 742-9.

Clark, E. V. (1972). On the child's acquisition of antonyms in two semantic fields. *Journal of Verbal Learning and Verbal Behavior*, **11**, 750-8.

Clark, E. V. (1973a). How children describe time and order. In Ferguson, C. A. and Slobin, D. I. (Eds.), *Studies of child language development*. New York: Holt, Rinehart and Winston.

Clark, E. V. (1973b). What's in a word? On the child's acquisition of semantics in his first language. In Moore, T. E. (Ed.), *Cognitive development and the acquisition of language*. New York: Academic Press.

Clark, E. V. (1973c). Non-linguistic strategies and the acquisition of word meanings. *Cognition*, **2**, 161-82.

Clark, E. V. (1974). Some aspects of the conceptual basis for first language acquisition. In Schiefelbusch, R. L. and Lloyd, L. L. (Eds.), *Language perspectives—acquisition, retardation and intervention*. Baltimore: University Park Press.

Clark, H. H. (1969). Linguistic processes in deductive reasoning. *Psychological Review*, **76**, 387-404.

Clark, H. H. (1970). The primitive nature of children's relational concepts. (Discussion of Donaldson and Wales). In Hayes, J. R. (Ed.), *Cognition and the development of language*. New York: Wiley.

Clark, H. H. (1973). Space, time, semantics and the child. In Moore, T. E. (Ed.), *Cognitive development and the acquisition of language*. New York: Academic Press.

Clark, H. H. and Clark, E. V. (1977). *Psychology and language*. New York: Harcourt Brace Jovanovich.

Cromer, R. F. (1970). 'Children are nice to understand': surface structure clues for the recovery of a deep structure. *British Journal of Psychology*, **61**, 397-408.

Cromer, R. F. (1972). The learning of surface structure clues to deep structure by a puppet show technique. *Quarterly Journal of Experimental Psychology*, **24**, 66-76.

Crystal, D. (1973). Non-segmental phonology in language acquisition: a review of the issues. *Lingua*, **32**, 1-45.

Danziger, K. (1957). The child's understanding of kinship terms: a study in the development of relational concepts. *Journal of Genetic Psychology*, **91**, 213-32.

Donaldson, M. and Balfour, G. (1968). Less is more: a study of language comprehension in children. *British Journal of Psychology*, **59**, 461-72.

Donaldson, M. and Wales, R. J. (1970). On the acquisition of relational terms. In Hayes, J. R. (Ed.), *Cognition and the development of language*. New York: Wiley.

Dore, J. (1973). The development of speech acts. Unpublished Ph.D. thesis, City University of New York.

Drach, K. (1968). The language of the parent: a pilot study. *Language, society and the child* (Working Paper No. 14), Language-Behavior Research Laboratory, University of California, Berkeley.

Eimas, P. D. (1975). Developmental studies of speech perception. In Cohen, L. B. and Salapatek, P. (Eds.), *Infant perception*. New York: Academic Press.

Eimas, P. D., Siqueland, E. R., Jusczyk, P. and Vigorito, J. (1971). Speech perception in infants. *Science*, **171**, 303-6.

Elkind, D. (1962). Children's conceptions of brother and sister: Piaget replication study V. *Journal of Genetic Psychology*, **100**, 129-36.

Ervin-Tripp, S. M. (1970). Discourse agreement: how children answer questions. In Hayes, J. R. (Ed.), *Cognition and the development of language*. New York: Wiley.

Ervin-Tripp, S. M. (1971). Social backgrounds and verbal skills. In Huxley, R. and Ingram, E. (Eds.), *Methods and models in language acquisition*. New York: Academic Press.

Ervin-Tripp, S. M. (1973). The structure of communicative choice. In Dil, A. S. (Ed.), *Language acquisition and communicative choice: essays by Susan M. Ervin-Tripp*. Stanford, Calif.: Stanford University Press.

Farwell, C. B. (1973). The language spoken to children. *Papers and Reports on Child Language Development*, Stanford University, **5**, 31-62.

Ferguson, C. A. and Garnica, O. K. (1975). Theories of phonological development. In Lenneberg, E. H. and Lenneberg, E. (Eds.), *Foundations of language development: a multidisciplinary approach*. New York: Academic Press.

Ferguson, C. A., Peizer, D. B. and Weeks, T. E. (1973). Model-and-replica phonological grammar of a child's first words. *Lingua*, **31**, 35-65.

Ferreiro, E. (1971). *Les relations temporelles dans le langage de l'enfant*. Genève: Droz.

Fillmore, C. J. (1968). The case for case. In Bach, E. and Harms, R. T. (Eds.), *Universals of linguistic theory*. New York: Holt, Rinehart and Winston.

Fillmore, C. J. (1971). Verbs of judging: an exercise in semantic description. In Fillmore, C. J. and Langendoen, D. T. (Eds.), *Studies in linguistic semantics*. New York: Holt, Rinehart and Winston.

Fodor, J. A. (1966). How to learn to talk: some simple ways. In Smith, F.

and Miller, G. A. (Eds.), *The genesis of language: a psycholinguistic approach*. Cambridge, Mass.: MIT Press.

Garnica, O. K. (1973). The development of phonemic speech perception. In Moore, T. E. (Ed.), *Cognitive development and the acquisition of language*. New York: Academic Press.

Garnica, O. K. (1975). Some characteristics of prosodic input to young children. Unpublished Ph.D. thesis, Stanford University.

Gelman, R. and Shatz, M. (1972). Listener-dependent adjustments in the speech of four-year-olds. Paper presented at the Pyschonomic Society Meeting, St Louis, Missouri.

Ghent, L. (1960). Recognition by children of realistic figures in various orientations. *Canadian Journal of Psychology*, **14**, 249-56.

Ghent Braine, L. (1972). The apparent upright—implications for copying and for perceptual development. Paper presented at the XXth International Congress of Psychology, Tokyo, Japan.

Gleitman, L. R., Gleitman, H. and Shipley, E. F. (1972). The emergence of the child as grammarian. *Cognition*, **1**, 137-64.

Gordon, D. and Lakoff, G. (1971). Conversational postulates. *Papers from the Seventh Regional Meeting, Chicago Linguistic Society*.

Greenberg, J. H. (1966). *Language universals*. The Hague: Mouton.

Greenfield, P. M., and Smith, J. H. (1976). *The structure of communication in early language development*. New York: Academic Press.

Grégoire, A. (1937, 1949). *L'apprentissage du langage*. (2 vols.) Paris: Droz.

Grice, H. P. (1967). Logic and conversation. Unpublished manuscript, William James Lectures, Harvard University.

Gruber, J. S. (1973). Correlations between the syntactic constructions of the child and the adult. In Ferguson, C. A. and Slobin, D. I. (Eds.), *Studies of child language development*. New York: Holt, Rinehart and Winston.

Guillaume, P. (1927/1973). Le développement des éléments formels dans le langage de l'enfant. *Journal de Psychologie*, **24**, 203-29. Translated in Ferguson, C. A. and Slobin, D. I. (Eds.), *Studies of child language development*. New York: Holt, Rinehart and Winston.

Gvozdev, A. N. (1961). *Voprosy izucheniya detskoy rechi*. Moscow: Akad. Pedag. Nauk RSFSR.

Halliday, M. A. K. (1970). Language structure and language function. In Lyons, J. (Ed.), *New horizons in linguistics*. Harmondsworth: Penguin Books.

Halliday, M. A. K. (1973). A sociosemiotic perspective on language development. Paper presented at the Fifth Child Language Research Forum, Stanford University.

Halliday, M. A. K. (1975). Learning how to mean. In Lenneberg, E. H. and Lenneberg, E. (Eds.), *Foundations of language development: a multidisciplinary approach*. New York: Academic Press.

Haviland, S. E. and Clark, E. V. (1974). 'This man's father is my father's son': a study of the acquisition of English kin terms. *Journal of Child Language*, **1**, 23-47.

Imedadze, N. V. (1960). K psikhologicheskoy prirode rannego dvuyazych- iya. *Voprosy Psikhologii*, **6**, 60-8.

Ingram, D. (1971). Transitivity in child language. *Language*, **47**, 888-910.

Jakobson, R. (1941/1968). *Kindersprache, Aphasie und allgemeine Lautgesetze*. (Uppsala, 1941). Translated: *Child language, aphasia and phonological universals*. The Hague: Mouton.

Jakobson, R. and Halle, M. (1956). *Fundamentals of language*. The Hague: Mouton.

Johnson, H. L. (1975). The meaning of *before* and *after* for preschool children. *Journal of Experimental Child Psychology*, **19**, 88-99.

Kaplan, E. L. (1969). The role of intonation in the acquisition of language. Unpublished Ph.D. thesis, Cornell University.

Kaplan, E. L. and Kaplan, G. A. (1970). The prelinguistic child. In Eliot, J. (Ed.), *Human development and cognitive processes*. New York: Holt, Rinehart and Winston.

Katz, J. J. and Fodor, J. A. (1963). The structure of a semantic theory. *Language*, **39**, 170-210.

Kessel, F. S. (1970). *The role of syntax in children's comprehension from ages six to twelve. Monographs of the Society for Research in Child Development*, **35**.

Klatzky, R. L., Clark, E. V. and Macken, M. (1973). Asymmetries in the acquisition of polar adjectives: linguistic or conceptual? *Journal of Experimental Child Psychology*, **16**, 32-46.

Klima, E. S. (1964). Negation in English. In Fodor, J. A. and Katz, J. J. (Eds.), *The structure of language*. Englewood Cliffs, N. J.: Prentice-Hall.

Klima, E. S. and Bellugi, U. (1966). Syntactic regularities in the speech of children. In Lyons, J. and Wales, R. J. (Eds.), *Psycholinguistics papers*. Edinburgh: Edinburgh University Press.

Kobashigawa, B. (1968). Repetitions in a mother's speech to her child. *Language, society and the child* (Working Paper No. 14), Language-Behavior Research Laboratory, University of California, Berkeley.

Kramer, P. E., Koff, E. and Luria, Z. (1972). The development of competence in an exceptional structure in older children and young adults. *Child Development*, **43**, 121-30.

Labov, W. (1970). The study of language in its social context. *Studium Generale*, **23**, 30-87.

Leech, G. N. (1970). *Towards a semantic description of English*. Bloomington, Ind.: Indiana University Press.

Leopold, W. F. (1949). *Speech development of a bilingual child*. Evanston, Ill.: Northwestern University Press.

Lewis, M. and Freedle, R. (1973). Mother-infant dyad: the cradle of meaning. In Pliner, P., Krames, L. and Alloway, T. (Eds.), *Communication and affect*. New York: Academic Press.

Lewis, M. M. (1936). *Infant speech: a study of the beginnings of language*. London: Routledge and Kegan Paul.

Lieberman, P. (1967). *Intonation, perception and language*. Cambridge, Mass.: MIT Press.

Limber, J. (1973). The genesis of complex sentences. In Moore, T. E. (Ed.), *Cognitive development and the acquisition of language.* New York: Academic Press.

Lyons, J. (1968). *Introduction to theoretical linguistics.* Cambridge: Cambridge University Press.

MacNamara, J. (1972). Cognitive basis of language learning in infants. *Psychological Review,* **79**, 1-13.

McCarthy, D. (1954). Language development in children. In Carmichael, L. (Ed.), *Manual of child psychology.* New York: Wiley.

McNeill, D. (1966). Developmental psycholinguistics. In Smith F. and Miller, G. A. (Eds.), *The genesis of language: a psycholinguistic approach.* Cambridge, Mass.: MIT Press.

McNeill, D. (1970). *The acquisition of language: the study of developmental psycholinguistics.* New York: Harper and Row.

McNeill, D. and McNeill, N. B. (1968). What does a child mean when he says 'No'? In Zale, E. M. (Ed.), *Proceedings of the Conference on Language and Language Behavior.* New York: Appleton-Century-Crofts.

Major, D. R. (1906). *First steps in mental growth.* New York: Macmillan Co.

Menn, L. (1971). Phonotactic rules in beginning speech: a study of the development of English discourse. *Lingua,* **26**, 225-51.

Menyuk, P. (1969). *Sentences children use.* Cambridge, Mass.: MIT Press.

Menyuk, P. and Bernholtz, N. (1969). Prosodic features and children's language production. *Research Laboratory of Electronics, Quarterly Research Reports,* MIT, **93**, 216-19.

Messer, S. (1967). Implicit phonology in children. *Journal of Verbal Learning and Verbal Behavior,* **6**, 609-13.

Moffitt, A. R. (1968). Speech perception by infants. Unpublished Ph.D. thesis, University of Minnesota.

Moffitt, A. R. (1971). Consonant cue perception by twenty- to twenty-four-week old infants. *Child Development,* **42**, 717-31.

Morse, P. A. (1972). The discrimination of speech and nonspeech stimuli in early infancy. *Journal of Experimental Child Psychology,* **14**, 477-92.

Morse, P. A. (1974). Infant speech perception: a preliminary model and review of the literature. In Schiefelbusch, R. L. and Lloyd, L. L. (Eds.), *Language perspectives—acquisition, retardation and intervention.* Baltimore, Md.: University Park Press.

Morton, J. and Smith, N. V. (1974). Some ideas concerning the acquisition of phonology. In *Proceedings of the Symposium on Current Problems in Psycholinguistics.* Paris: CNRS.

Moscowitz, A. I. (1970). The two-year-old stage in the acquisition of English phonology. *Language,* **46**, 426-41.

Moscowitz, A. I. (1971). The acquisition of phonology. Unpublished Ph.D. thesis, University of California, Berkeley.

Mowrer, O. H. (1960). *Learning theory and symbolic processes.* New York: Wiley.

Nelson, K. (1972). Semantic structures of the earliest lexicons. Paper presented at the Eastern Psychological Association meeting, Boston, Mass.

Öhman, S. (1953). Theories of the 'linguistic field'. *Word*, 9, 123-4.

Omar, M. K. (1970). The acquisition of Egyptian Arabic as a native language. Unpublished Ph.D. thesis, Georgetown University.

Palermo, D. S. (1973). More about less: a study of language comprehension. *Journal of Verbal Learning and Verbal Behavior*, 12, 211-21.

Perez, B. (1892). *Les trois premières années de l'enfant*. Paris: Alcan.

Phillips, J. R. (1973). Syntax and vocabulary of mothers' speech to young children: age and sex comparisons. *Child Development*, 44, 182-5.

Piaget, J. (1928). *Judgment and reasoning in the child*. London: Routledge and Kegan Paul.

Postal, P. M. (1966). Review article: Martinet André, *Elements of general linguistics*. *Foundations of Language*, 2, 151-86.

Romney, A. K. and D'Andrade, R. G. (1964). Cognitive aspects of English kin terms. *American Anthropologist*, 66, 146-70.

Ross, J. R. (1970). On declarative sentences. In Jacobs, R. A. and Rosenbaum, P. S. (Eds.), *Readings in English transformational grammar*. Waltham, Mass.: Ginn and Co.

Rūke-Draviņa, V. (1959/1973). Zur Entstehung der Flexion in der Kindersprache: Ein Beitrag auf der Grundlage des littischen Sprachmateriels. *International Journal of Slavic Linguistics and Poetics*, 1/2, 201-22. Translated in Ferguson, C. A. and Slobin, D. I. (Eds.), *Studies of child language development*. New York: Holt, Rinehart and Winston.

Sachs, J. S., Brown, R. and Salerno, R. A. (1972). Adults' speech to children. Paper presented at the International Symposium on First Language Acquisition, Florence, Italy.

Schlesinger, I. M. (1971). Production of utterances and language acquisition. In Slobin, D. I. (Ed.), *The ontogenesis of grammar: a theoretical symposium*. New York: Academic Press.

Schlesinger, I. M. (1974). Relational concepts underlying language. In Schiefelbusch, R. L. and Lloyd, L. L. (Eds.), *Language perspectives— acquisition, retardation and intervention*. Baltimore, Md.: University Park Press.

Searle, J. R. (1970). *Speech acts: an essay in the philosophy of language*. Cambridge: Cambridge University Press.

Searle, J. R. (Ed.) (1971). *The philosophy of language*. Oxford: Oxford University Press.

Shatz, M. and Gelman, R. (1973). *The development of communication skills: modifications in the speech of young children as a function of listener*. *Monographs of the Society for Research in Child Development*, 38.

Sheldon, A. L. (1972). The acquisition of relative clauses in English. Unpublished Ph.D. thesis, University of Texas.

Shipley, E. F., Smith, C. S. and Gleitman, L. R. (1969). A study in the acquisition of language: free responses to commands. *Language*, 45, 322-42.

Schvachkin, N. Kh. (1948/1973). Razvitiye fonematicheskogo vospriyatiya rechi v rannem vozraste. *Izvestiya Akad. Pedag. Nauk RSFSR*, **13**, 101-32. Translated in Ferguson, C. A. and Slobin, D. I. (Eds.), *Studies of child language development*. New York: Holt, Rinehart and Winston.

Sinclair-de Zwart, H. (1967). *Acquisition du langage et développement de la pensée: Sous-systèmes linguistiques et opérations concrètes*. Paris: Dunod.

Sinclair-de Zwart, H. (1969). Developmental psycholinguistics. In Elkind, D. and Flavell, J. H. (Eds.), *Studies in cognitive development*. London: Oxford University Press.

Sinclair, H. and Ferreiro, E. (1970). Etude génétique de la compréhension, production et répétition des phrases au mode passif. *Archives de Psychologie*, **40**, 1-42.

Slobin, D. I. (1966a). Grammatical transformations and sentence comprehension in childhood and adulthood. *Journal of Verbal Learning and Verbal Behavior*, **5**, 219-27.

Slobin, D. I. (1966b). The acquisition of Russian as a native language. In Smith, F. and Miller, G. A. (Eds.), *The genesis of language: a psycholinguistic approach*. Cambridge, Mass.: MIT Press.

Slobin, D. I. (1970). Universals of grammatical development in children. In Flores d'Arcais, G. B. and Levelt, W. J. M. (Eds.), *Advances in psycholinguistics*. Amsterdam: North-Holland Publishing Co.

Slobin, D. I. (1973). Cognitive prerequisites for the development of grammar. In Ferguson, C. A. and Slobin, D. I. (Eds.), *Studies of child language development*. New York: Holt, Rinehart and Winston.

Slobin, D. I. and Welsh, C. A. (1973). Elicited imitation as a research tool in developmental psycholinguistics. In Ferguson, C. A. and Slobin, D. I. (Eds.), *Studies of child language development*. New York: Holt, Rinehart and Winston.

Smith, C. S. (1970). An experimental approach to children's linguistic competence. In Hayes, J. R. (Ed.), *Cognition and the development of language*. New York: Wiley.

Smith, N. V. (1973). *The acquisition of phonology: a case study*. Cambridge: Cambridge University Press.

Snow, C. E. (1972a). Mothers' speech to children learning language. *Child Development*, **43**, 549-65.

Snow C. E. (1972b). Young children's responses to adult sentences of varying complexity. Paper presented at the Third International Congress of Applied Linguistics, Copenhagen, Denmark.

Spears, W. C. and Hohle, R. H. (1967). Sensory and perceptual processes in infants. In Brackbill, Y. (Ed.), *Infancy and early childhood*. New York: The Free Press.

Stern, W. (1930). *Psychology of early childhood*. New York: Holt.

Tonkova-Yampol'skaya, R. V. (1969). Development of speech intonation in infants during the first two years of life. *Soviet Psychology*, **7**, 48-54.

Wallace, A. F. C. and Atkins, J. (1960). The meaning of kinship terms. *American Anthropologist*, **62**, 58-79.

Waterson, N. (1971). Child phonology: a prosodic view. *Journal of Linguistics*, 7, 179-211.

Watt, W. C. (1970). Comments on the Brown and Hanlon paper. In Hayes, J. R. (Ed.), *Cognition and the development of language*. New York: Wiley.

Weir, R. H. (1962). *Language in the crib*. The Hague: Mouton.

Wertheimer, M. (1961). Psychomotor coordination of auditory and visual space at birth. *Science*, 134, 1692.

Wolff, P. H. (1963). Observations on the early development of smiling. In Foss, B. M. (Ed.), *Determinants of infant behavior*, vol. 2. New York: Wiley.

Wolff, P. H. (1966). The natural history of crying and other vocalizations in early infancy. In Foss, B. M. (Ed.), *Determinants of infant behavior*, vol. 4. New York: Wiley.

The Regulatory Function of Language

An analysis and contribution to the current controversy over the Soviet theory

DAVID BLOOR
Lecturer in Science Studies, University of Edinburgh

74

CONTENTS

Soviet researchers have concerned themselves more with the function of language than with its structure. Their question has been: what does language enable human beings to do that they could not do without it? The slogan which sums up the answer given by A. R. Luria and his co-workers is that language is the means whereby humans learn to regulate their own behaviour. My use of the word 'slogan' is deliberate. The claim that language has a regulatory function is not a single and explicit theory but an overall perspective. Its meaning has to be gathered from a diverse range of illustrative experiments.

First, I will try to convey the meaning of the regulatory thesis. Second, I will review some American work which has conspicuously failed to replicate the results of Soviet psychologists. Third, this scientific controversy will be analysed in the light of a striking claim by R. H. Wozniak (1972) that the whole affair is based on a complex theoretical cum cultural misunderstanding. The questions to be considered must be: are Soviet and American researchers really disagreeing with one another, or are their approaches, techniques and theories so different that the replications simply by-pass the claims that they are supposed to be testing? The answer that I will give is that although Wozniak's approach represents a marked advance in the theoretical sophistication with which Soviet work is approached, nevertheless it fails as a satisfying defence against the accumulated experimental evidence. Finally, some of the more positive aspects of the affair will be drawn together. I shall claim that the most reliable experimental results which we possess can best be treated by the theoretical idea of limited channel capacity. This theory is one which no worker in the field, Russian or American, has previously used. The claims for the value of this approach will be substantiated by experiments which have not previously been published.[1]

1. I should like to acknowledge the very valuable advice and comments contributed by the editors, John Morton and John Marshall, and also by Ruth Clarke. The remaining obscurities and errors are, of course, my own.

THE BACKGROUND OF SOVIET EXPERIMENTS ON REGULATION

In order to make clear the content of the thesis that language regulates behaviour I shall go back to the earliest available translated source of Luria's ideas—his book *The Nature of Human Conflicts* (1932). It is something of a mystery that this source is hardly ever mentioned by those who have worked on Luria's ideas.

Luria's picture of brain function is one which lays great stress on the emergence within the brain of two distinct but interacting parts or systems. One part contains highly elaborated, very labile interconnections. Indeed it embodies and mirrors all the complexity of the concepts which are derived from the language, culture and education of the subject. For simplicity this can be called the 'verbal system'. The other part of the brain is much simpler and is thought to function rather like the non-human brain. It begins life with a limited repertoire of reflexes which are elaborated by classical conditioning. Stimulation of the sense-organs causes excitation to surge across this lower centre. In the normal course of events any excitation finds its outlet by triggering a response in the motor system. Should stimulation call forth antagonistic responses, the collisions of excitation are reflected in the outer disorganisation of behaviour.

This lower centre lacks what the Pavlovians call 'mobility'. It cannot move from one sequence of reflexes to another in accord with an abstract strategy which is not present in the stimulus situation. According to Luria disorganization, confusion and conflict are held at bay by the influence of the more sophisticated system. This interposes itself as a 'functional barrier' between stimulus and response. The proper functioning of the adult brain takes place when all stimuli are channelled through the 'verbal system' before discharging into the motor system.

This picture has three important facets. First, child development is the story of the individual's construction of a functional barrier—an achievement in which social and educational influences are paramount. The social aspects of the theory are derived from the work of L. S. Vygotsky (1962). Second, arrested development and nervous illness are invariably accompanied by a disturbance of the functional barrier. Pathological states such as neuroses are characteristically seen by Luria as resulting from an excess of sub-cortical excitation. This bursts through the functional barrier expressing itself in disorganized action and emotion. Conversely, various forms of retardation stem from the inability of the higher centres to impose constraint on otherwise normal amounts of excitation. Third, despite Luria's vivid imagery of the 'barrier' between the two systems, he also stresses the 'dialectical' relation between them. The two systems interact and continuously modify one another. They exemplify the law of the interpenetration and unity of opposites. Luria believes that as a consequence not so much as the crooking of a finger is devoid of participation by linguistic and cultural components. As he puts it, 'the limits of speech are not where we are accustomed to see them' (1932, p. 389).

So much for the overall structure of the theory. Luria fills out the picture with evidence both general and particular. The general considerations are easy to appreciate. It has seemed to many investigators that there is a qualitative difference between the ways in which animals learn and the way human adults master tasks. In a laboratory, animal learning frequently exhibits a slow development dependent on sustained rewards. The learning when achieved is specific to the training situation and unresponsive to changes in the environment which may require alteration of the learnt behaviour patterns. Adult humans by contrast are known to approach, say a discrimination task, in an analytical and questioning way. They actively search out a rule to follow and are often capable of revising the rule in order to meet changed circumstances.

Language seems to be an obvious way of explaining this difference. Humans learn by verbally formulating a rule which sums up the problem situation and guides future responses. Luria belongs to a tradition going back at least as far as Descartes when he appeals to language in this way. But human adult skills differ in these characteristic ways not only from animals, but from children too. Here again the possession of language seems to correlate in an illuminating way. This poses Luria with the problem of understanding the development of verbal regulation. Here it is necessary to move from his early work to the later publications, for example, *The Role of Speech in the Regulation of Normal and Abnormal Behaviour* (1962). With the exception of one theoretical innovation, to be discussed later, the continuity of method and theory is striking.

Luria's experiments have led him to postulate three stages of development. For children around one-and-a-half to three-years old the verbal control of behaviour resides with adults who direct the child's attention and issue commands. At this stage commands can initiate actions but not inhibit them. A child who is told to put his socks on may oblige. If he is told to take them off again when the action is under way the command is more likely to act as encouragement than to produce the desired reversal.

For children from three to between four and five years verbal control is still at first largely provided by adults, but their speech is now able to inhibit action as well as to initiate it. This second stage is the one more intensively studied by Luria. It is a transitional period where he believes it is possible to show the beginnings of verbal self-regulation. Before moving on to the final stage some of his more important experiments will be discussed.

Luria's typical experimental approach consists in presenting his child subjects with a sequence of light signals and giving them a verbal instruction to press a small rubber bulb when the signals occur. Sometimes more than one colour of light signal is used, only one of the two requiring a response. The pressure of the child's hand as well as the occurrence of the stimuli are recorded on a kymograph. This makes it possible to tell whether responses have been missed or if extra responses have been made. Pictures of the peaked and wavy traces of the response curve are characteristic features of Luria's books. In his early work especially, he analyses these pictures in great detail, reading off from them the state of the hidden processes in the brain.

In his experiments Luria found that children up to two years old begin to press the bulb as soon as they are given the instructions. They cannot wait for the lights. At a later age children can be trained to wait for the signals. Even then, they are prone to 'perseverate', that is, to produce many inter-signal pressures. Good co-ordination of signals and responses can be achieved in two-and-a-half to three-year olds by a variety of means. One way is to accompany every signal by a direct instruction from an adult. Another way is to make the response produce a clear feedback signal, say, sounding a bell or switching off the stimulus light. A third way is to instruct the child to press the rubber bulb and then put his hand on his knee until the next signal.

These methods work, Luria argues, because they provide a source of stimulation after the response has been made. This sets up a fresh surge of excitation which collides with that already set up in the brain by the first stimulus. The original excitation is blocked and contained, thus preventing it from producing uncontrolled perseveration of the response.

Luria believes that the role played by the external source of excitation provided by the adult, the feedback or the 'double start' in the above experiments, can be taken over by the child's own verbal system. This depends on the verbal system having achieved a greater degree of organization than the motor system itself. Without this there would be no hope of the one being able to help improve the workings of the other. It is now clear just how much Luria's later work still depends on his earlier stress on the different natures of the two brain systems. If the brain were completely undifferentiated and uniform in its workings and development there would be no room for an explanation of this form.

The unequal ability of the verbal and motor systems is demonstrated by an experiment in which the purely verbal reaction of saying 'go!' is given to the light signals. Children of three to four years can perform this task with no verbal perseveration or confusion, even though they cannot perform the simple corresponding motor task of pressing a bulb. The verbal and motor systems can then be brought into contact with one another by asking the child to press the bulb at the same time as saying 'go'. Children of two to two-and-a-half years cannot perform both tasks at once. But for three- to four-year olds the result is that the motor performance improves. It is regulated by the verbal system.

What is held to be going on in the brain that accounts for this regulation? As previously outlined the diffuse excitation caused by sensory stimulation is diverted into the verbal system. The verbal system acts like a gate holding the excitation in check—hence the name 'functional barrier'. The internal connections of the verbal system regulate the flow of excitation so that the stimulation reaches the motor system at the precise moment and with the precise energy required to trigger specific motor responses. What is it that determines the opening and closing of the gate to achieve this result? This is done by the child's saying 'go!', hence the timing and frequency of the motor response is controlled by the verbal behaviour.

The developmental story is far from complete at this stage. The child has now achieved a form of autonomous verbal self-regulation, but the level at which it works is rather elementary. Luria says that it is merely the existence of the verbal response as a source of excitation, rather than the meaning of the word which acts as a regulator. To show this he performs another experiment of combining the verbal and motor systems (1961, p. 57). Here children are asked to press a rubber bulb for one colour of signal but not for the other. They are also asked to say 'press' and 'don't press' appropriately. The result is that saying 'don't press' has exactly the same result as saying 'press'. Merely uttering the word helps trigger the motor response, even though its meaning forbids it. If the children are asked to say 'press' merely for those signals requiring a response, but to say nothing at all for the others, the difficulty disappears. At this stage, according to Luria, speech is working by means of its 'impulsive aspect' rather than via its meaning.

The transfer of control from the impulsive aspect to the meaning of words represents a third and final stage in development. This takes place between four-and-a-half and five years of age. Saying a word or sentence now opens specific gates in the functional barrier and produces or inhibits correspondingly specific responses. A red button is pressed because the child says 'press red' or just 'red'. Unfortunately Luria says very little about this transition. Detailed mechanisms are not spelled out. The situation is also complicated by the fact that at precisely this age verbal control is said to pass from overt to covert speech.

Before examining further experimental evidence bearing on the regulatory function of language, a sweeping theoretical objection deserves examination. Luria's account of the verbal regulation of motor responses is an explanation of one skill by appeal to another: skill A is explained by skill B; subjects can do A because they can first do B. But don't explanations of this type fall into an infinite regress? Surely such accounts merely postpone explanatory problems.

Broadbent makes a similar point when considering the superiority of humans over, say, monkeys, in learning to produce preplanned sequences of responses, e.g., undoing a set of locks in a certain order. He rejects the idea that humans are good at this task because they can verbally formulate the sequence they are to adopt. 'From the present point of view', he says, 'this is putting the cart before the horse . . .' (1958, p.47). People are not good at sequences *because* of their verbal skills; this explanation would still leave unanswered the problem of the origin of the verbal skills. Rather, they are good at sequences because of their large nervous systems and this in turn explains their verbal ability. Stated generally Broadbent's point is that language is part of the output of behaviour which constitutes the psychologist's problem rather than being part of his kit of ultimate solutions.

How devastating is this objection to the regulatory view of language? Clearly it imposes some important limitations. Language cannot be an unexplained explainer, so Luria's theory is not dealing with first principles. If language does indeed regulate, the question can still be asked: what regulates language? But even if the theory does not raise the deepest questions it can still deal with important intermediate issues about the relations and dispositions of the brain's subsystems. This is exactly the area with which Luria concerns himself when he analyses the brain into different functional systems. It is perfectly in order to hold that one of these, say the verbal system, has greater information processing capacity than the other, and that this capacity is exploited by stimuli being channelled through it. To this extent it is legitimate to invoke the verbal system when explaining the other parts of the brain. Viewed in this way the regulatory theory can survive the threat raised by the infinite regress argument implicit in Broadbent's position.

A more immediate threat lies in the fact that American psychologists have tried to replicate the experiments of Luria's described above—and they have failed.

AMERICAN ATTEMPTS AT REPLICATION

I shall now summarise three experiments which were intended to replicate Luria's results. In all cases the authors report a complete failure.[1] The important assumptions behind the experiments will be left for the next section.

Jarvis (1963) conducted an investigation to test Luria's hypothesis that there is 'a stage of development during which instructing a child to verbalize . . . to give himself instructions . . . whilst performing a sensory-motor task, will improve his performance if he tells himself what to do, but hinder his performance if he tells himself what not to do'.

His subjects were instructed to push a button whenever they saw a blue light but refrain from pushing when they saw a yellow light. The stimuli consisted of a random sequence of 30 blue and 20 yellow lights. The signals lasted half a second with an interstimulus interval of three-quarters of a second.

There were three experimental conditions: (1) a *silent* condition; (2) a *push* condition in which subjects said 'push' when they saw a blue light and pushed; (3) a *don't push* condition in which subjects said 'don't push' whenever they saw a yellow light. Four groups of subjects were used (mean ages in months, $46 \cdot 8$, $59 \cdot 5$, $71 \cdot 6$, $80 \cdot 7$). Each of the 72 subjects was given all three conditions in an order counter-balanced across each group.

Jarvis' results did not support Luria's hypothesis. They showed that the child's ability to perform the experimental task improved with age, but verbalization, or the lack of it, had no significant effect on their performance.

Similar negative results were found by Wilder (1968) with experiments which again used repeated measure designs but much smaller numbers of subjects. One of his experiments (N=14) directly compared silent responding with combined motor and verbal responding when three- and five-year olds are given a single stimulus, bulb pressing task. Luria would predict that for children over three years old performance would improve. For the five-year

1.   There is another experiment by Joynt and Cambourne (1968) where the authors conclude that their work supports Luria. Along with others I do not see how this conclusion is reached. A detailed discussion is to be found in Miller, Shelton and Flavell (1970) and Wozniak (1972).

olds verbal control should be covert, so that speech would not be expected to improve performance: indeed it might interfere.

The results were that the five-year olds showed a smaller and more stable latency and made fewer omissions. The five-year olds also showed more stability in the amplitude of their responses when they vocalized. There was no evidence that speech helped the three-year olds or that it hindered the five-year olds.

One trend which Wilder remarked upon was that the three-year olds in the vocalization condition tended to vocalize on trials in which pressing responses were omitted. As Wilder puts it, 'speech tended to replace the hand-squeeze response . . . rather than to facilitate it' (p.430).

Another experiment to test the developmental claims of the regulatory theory is by Miller, Shelton and Flavell (1970). They avoided the use of a repeated measure design lest carry-over effects were responsible for blurring the regulatory phenomenon that was being sought.

Subjects were again given a typical Luria task of making motor responses to a sequence of light signals. The stimuli were 20 blue and 20 yellow signals each lasting one second with about two seconds between them. One colour, designated positive, required the response of pressing a rubber bulb. The other colour, designated negative, did not require a motor response.

Four experimental conditions varied the verbal response. These were: (1) silent responding; (2) saying 'squeeze' to a positive stimulus; (3) saying 'don't squeeze' to a negative stimulus; (4) verbalization to both positive and negative stimuli.

Each subject was given just one of the four conditions and four different age groups were used. Each group contained 20 boys and 20 girls. The mean ages of the groups were 3;2, 3;7, 4;12 and 4;11 in years and months.

The developmental hypotheses tested in this experiment were that at about three years the motor task should be performed best during silent responding. At three and a half verbalization should have an impulsive effect, helping the responses to a positive stimulus but interfering with the inhibition required by the negative stimulus. By four, verbalization should equally improve the positive and negative trials. The final developmental stage corresponds to the internalization of verbal self-control, so that overt verbalization should have no effect on motor responding.

In the author's words:

The results stand in clear contradiction to the developmental changes predicted from Luria's hypothesis. Among children who were the same ages as those employed by Luria, there is no indication of a nonsemantic, impelling effect of the child's speech on his motor activity, nor is there any evidence for improved motor performance due to the semantic content of the self-instruction. There is little evidence, in fact, that overt self-instructions have any effect on behaviour in this task at any of the four ages sampled. (p. 662)

One of the subsidiary conclusions of this experiment is of great interest. It was found that for the youngest subjects the response to the positive stimulus was often disrupted when they were required to verbalize. The authors conclude that:

the two responses seem better viewed as two independent tasks . . . Rather than a useful mediator, the verbalization of 'squeeze' was merely a second thing for the child to do. (p. 664)

WOZNIAK'S ATTEMPT AT RAPPROCHEMENT

The broad outlines of the controversy are clear. An extensive Soviet tradition of work extending back many years has been called into question by a small number of rigorous American experiments.

Nobody who reads the works in question can fail to be struck by the differences in national style. The two lines of work are grounded in quite different theories. The physiological and clinical orientation of the Soviet work emerges in their use of the representative case, rather than the experimental group which is the American unit of analysis. The presentation and processing of data also conform to quite different standards. Some observers may draw the ethnocentric conclusion that the dispute is simply a case of good science versus bad science. Seen in this way the controversy can be quickly resolved: the American work is right and there is no good evidence for language having a regulatory function.

R. H. Wozniak's response is far more sophisticated. He believes that the two traditions of work have not properly made contact. The open texture of the Soviet research may have uncovered an area of human performance which eludes the stereotyped demands of an unimaginatively applied conception of experimental rigour.

Part of his argument consists in stressing the fact that Soviet work rests on marxist philosophical assumptions. It is shot through with dialectical thinking of a sort alien to American research. This is surely correct. Luria's early work provides a rather more pointed example than the ones Wozniak gives. This lies in the idea of the brain containing qualitatively different parts rather than being a mechanical accumulation of similar elements such as reflex arcs.

Luria expects to find different but interacting principles of operation at work when he deals with different levels of performance. This
is a theoretical 'set' which can plausibly be attributed to the cultural
background of his work.

The difference between the conception of brain function as
qualitatively varying rather than uniform and cumulative highlights
the misunderstanding embodied in the American assumption that
Luria's theory is a version of S-R mediation theory. Mediation
theory comes to terms with language by seeing it as merely a special
case of the usual S-R mechanisms. Verbal processes are simply overt
or covert responses to an external stimulus. These responses set up
their own stimulation and the final response is now made to the new
array of stimulation. The laws governing these mediating processes
are the same as for any other stimulus or response. Clearly any
attempt to equate the mediation and regulatory theories will ride
roughshod over the more dialectical aspects of the Russian version.

Does anything important follow from ignoring the difference?
Wozniak thinks that it does. For mediation theory language is
simply a source of stimuli. Self-regulation is equated with self-
stimulation. The verbal system has only one function—it *elicits*
responses. Wozniak stresses that this ignores what the Soviet
psychologists say about language's role in inhibiting responses. For
Wozniak the equation with mediation theory distorts the conduct
of the American work. The equation even influences the experimental designs used in the American work, and so the misunderstanding is built into the very texture of their investigations. This
shows itself in the way in which Wilder, Jarvis and Miller *et al.*
specifically request their child subjects to vocalize before responding. They do this because they want the motor response to be
brought forth or stimulated by the verbal response.

Wozniak's reading of the Russian theory is that just as asking a
child to press the bulb *and then* put his hand on his knee helps stop
perseveration so does his pressing *and then* saying 'go!'. If the
American experimenters had interpreted the Russian theory as
meaning that language regulates by this sort of inhibition they would
never have imposed on their subjects the conditions that they did.

Two facts are adduced by Wozniak to support this central feature
of his argument. First, it was clear from the American experiments
that, despite their instructions, the children were prone to reverse
the required order of responding. They tended to make the manual
response and then speak. Second, Wozniak believes that requiring
a child to speak first will set up an orienting response which will
inhibit the subsequent pressing movement that he was meant to have
produced. The mechanism of inhibition which would normally

stop perseveration will, under these conditions, simply inhibit all motor responses. He cites as evidence for this the observation of Wilder that many of his subjects were prone to stop responding and either pressed or spoke but not both.

Wozniak argues that apart from this theoretical and experimental misunderstanding the replications contain another fundamental error. This derives from the taken-for-granted norms of the American researchers regarding instructions and warm-up procedures. It is standard practice to devise experimental tasks requiring complex instructions. These are given to the subject at the beginning of the experiment and, to ensure that they have been mastered, warm-up and practice trials are a frequent preliminary to the experiment proper. Wozniak insists that this is not the only scientific way of proceeding. It is just as legitimate to be interested in spontaneous levels of performance rather than in those given by subjects who have been trained up to some arbitrary criterion. Similarly the building up of the understanding of the instructions is itself a subject worthy of study. It is a transitory developmental process which is presupposed by many experiments and yet at the same time rendered well-nigh invisible. Pre-training procedures may lift subjects above the level where manipulating the verbal responses makes any difference. It is perhaps these fluid, evanescent phases of social learning that have captured the attention of Soviet researchers.

Wozniak then delineates a third source of misunderstanding which again derives from the different procedural norms of Russian and American psychologists. It concerns the American assumption that a uniform and mechanical imposition of stimuli on the subject is of the essence of good experimental technique. Shouldn't the rate of presentation be adjusted to fit the characteristics of the subject? If this is not done then the stimulus situation may be perceived and responded to differently by different types of subjects. Where is objectivity then? What concerns Wozniak particularly is that the rate at which stimuli were presented in some of the replications, for example that of Jarvis, was so fast that there was no chance that perseveration could show itself. If verbal regulation is the inhibition of perseveration, then no wonder it was not captured by this replication.

The final phase of Wozniak's defence of the regulatory theory consists in his reviewing a number of experiments which he believes provide indirect evidence in support of Luria. This work is done within a Skinnerian framework but is seen by its authors as well as by Wozniak to bear on the Soviet theory. The experiments combine verbal and motor tasks. The idea is that the performance of the motor task will vary in ways which depend on the accompanying verbal output, thus giving a measure of verbal regulation. In order to avoid simply repeating reviews of the literature a single experiment will be selected as an example. This is Meichenbaum and Goodman's study 'The developmental control of operant motor responding by verbal operants' (1969). It amply illustrates the character of this body of work and will provide the opportunity to show Wozniak's general line of reasoning in assessing its significance for Luria.

Leaving aside the details of the experimental procedure, Meichenbaum and Goodman found that children between five and seven years tapped at a different rate when they were asked to repeat a word, than when they tapped silently. Furthermore the rate varied with what they were asked to repeat. If the word's meaning was irrelevant to the task, like 'letter', it slowed down the rate of tapping from the silent condition. If asked to repeat the word 'faster', tapping speeded up from the base-line of irrelevant vocalization, whereas repeating the word 'slower' slowed the tapping down from this rate. The experiment was repeated with other children merely being asked to mouth or whisper the words rather than say them aloud. This was found to produce exactly the same pattern of results. The age of the subjects and the effects of the overt or covert style of vocalization were found to be linked in an interesting way. Saying 'faster' or 'slower' always produced the appropriate variation from the rate of tapping with irrelevant vocalization. But for the older children saying 'faster' still did not produce tapping as fast as the purely silent condition. This was only achieved by the older children when they accompanied their tapping by whispered responses. For the younger children the opposite relation held. They could only rival their silent tapping rate when repeating the word 'faster' aloud, but not when whispering it.

More will be said about this experiment below, where particular attention will be paid to the instructions given to the subjects. The point to retain for the moment is that Wozniak sees the results as supporting Luria in two ways. First, the differential effect of whispered responses is seen as an instance of the internalization of verbal self-regulation. It is held to show the regulating effect passing into internal speech—assuming that whispering is a step towards internal speech. That the experiment does indeed yield genuine cases of verbal self-regulation is not questioned. The second way in which the experiment is held to favour Luria arises from the fact that it shows that sometimes the child's speech actually interferes with the rate of tapping. To see how this can be read as positive evidence for Luria, it is necessary to remember that Wozniak believes that regulation consists in the verbal inhibition of perseveration:

Such an interference effect in a manual task which is discrete (i.e., a finger tap) to the extent that it implies that the function of a child's verbal response is not always facilitative, supports the existence of the verbal inhibition of a continuous manual response (i.e., a bulb squeeze) as reported by Luria. (Wozniak, p. 49)

I have now outlined in some detail both sides of the dispute over the regulatory function of language as well as a determined attempt to resolve the conflict and show that indirect evidence in fact supports Luria's case. The problem is what to make of this dialectic of thesis, antithesis and synthesis.

A 'CAPACITY' THEORY

How badly does the American work miss the point of the Soviet theory? There is no doubt that some of Wozniak's criticisms strike home. The perseveration of motor responses which is one of the main symptoms of lack of motor regulation is unlikely to show itself if stimuli are presented too rapidly. The requirement that verbal responses precede motor responses is, again, something never found in the Soviet experiments. These points, combined with the observations about pre-training, will contribute substantially to improving the focus of future experiments.

But is it really the case, as Wozniak asserts, that the Soviet theory is completely based on mechanisms of inhibition? I believe that this is to misunderstand Luria's theory and that, when the record is put straight, the failed replications can once more be seen to pose genuine problems for the regulatory theory.

When Luria's theory is placed in the context of his 1932 writings the limitation of Wozniak's account becomes clear because the verbal system is not only responsible for inhibiting motor responses but also for eliciting or producing them. It is indeed true that the verbal system as a whole constitutes a general source of inhibition. The functional barrier stops excitation irradiating in an uncontrolled way from the sense-organs to the motor outlets.

Between the stimulus and the reaction in the adult lies a certain regulating mechanism which causes a corresponding transfer of excitation to the motor path, but does not admit to the motor system the whole quantity of excitation which was produced by the stimulus. (Luria, 1932, p.342)

But this is not the whole story. Making specific verbal responses opens gates in the functional barrier in order to produce particular motor responses. In this sense the motor responses are elicited or prompted by speech. To change the metaphor: saying 'go!' punches a hole in the functional barrier. Both the inhibition and the releasing or eliciting of motor responses are characteristic of the overall operation of the verbal system. As Luria expresses it in his later work, language first possesses an initiating function, then it achieves an inhibitory role. Regulation proper is a *synthesis* of these two elements (1951, p.29). To stress one aspect of this synthesis at the expense of the other is to miss the whole point.

Wozniak's interpretation cannot do justice to what Luria says about the role of speech as a form of auto-stimulation. In discussing a case of Parkinson's disease Luria says:

> If the application of speech can help to inhibit the impulsive movements, then in the cases where the control of movement means acceleration, in the overcoming of organic rigidity, language may serve as a psychological compensation for the motor defects. In our experiments with paralysis agitans we attempt to show whether a word can act as a stimulating agent just as the external motor stimulus did. (1932, p.413)

The American replications may indeed have paid too little attention to the inhibition of perseveration but they still provided an opportunity for the verbal prompting and timing of motor responses to show itself—an effect which failed to materialize.

How could the one-sided, inhibition interpretation of Luria have arisen? The main reason is probably lack of familiarity with his book *Human Conflicts.* In his later works the concept of the functional barrier is less in evidence. Indeed the label has been completely dropped, but it was seen above that the concept still structures Luria's theory. Another explanation is that the later work grafts onto the earlier theory a number of fashionable cybernetic analogies. These make it difficult to bring the overall structure of the theory into focus. In a distracting way they are never rendered fully commensurable with it.[1]

What is to be made of the indirect evidence of the Skinnerian work which is said to support the regulatory thesis? Wozniak's handling of Meichenbaum and Goodman's findings went like this: Luria's theory of verbal regulation is a theory of inhibition. The

---

1.   Luria is an eclectic theory builder and the hope of reconciling all of the things that he says about his theory may be a vain one. Clarity is perhaps best served by sharply separating the Pavlovian and cybernetic elements of his account. The outcome of Wozniak's detailed attempts to come to terms with Luria's cybernetic ideas reinforces me in this conclusion.

experimental data reveals that verbal responses can interfere with motor responses. Interference is a form of inhibition, therefore the experiments support Luria's theory.

This argument is logically valid but it is a very weak form of confirmation. The issue which has to be clarified before the strength of the indirect evidence can be assessed is whether the *kind* of inhibition postulated by Luria's regulatory theory is indeed the kind of inhibition which has been observed by Meichenbaum and Goodman. If they are not of the same kind, then the experiments will turn out to provide no support at all for the regulatory theory.

I believe that the interference observed by Meichenbaum and Goodman can best be considered to derive from the fact that the verbal task imposes a load on the motor task and that the motor and verbal systems are competing for the limited resources of the nervous system. If this claim can be supported by independent evidence then the picture which it suggests is quite different from Luria's. Rather than the motor system being controlled by the verbal system the two can be considered to be quite independent of one another, except in so far as they are competing for limited channel capacity. From now on this intuitively simple model will be called the 'capacity theory'.

Consider again Meichenbaum and Goodman's findings. Children tapped faster when they repeated the word 'faster'. What was the base line here? It was in fact the rate of the child's tapping when he had no speed at all suggested to him—in particular, when he was not told to tap rapidly. Was it the child's repetition of the word 'faster' which caused the increase in speed? This is doubtful because the experimental instructions required the child to tap 'the way the word means'. In short he was told to tap rapidly. It transpires that this is not a case of self-regulation in which the child's verbal system plays a controlling part. It is simply a demonstration of the fact that children can obey an instruction to tap rapidly or slowly at the same time as obeying the instruction to repeat a word. It is not surprising that the child can produce tapping which is either faster or slower than the base line when he is requested to do so.

The question now arises of what would have happened if the fast verbally accompanied tapping had been compared with a silent base line of fast tapping, i.e. where the child has been told to tap rapidly. I have performed this simple experiment and the result is very clear. For children around six years old silent fast tapping is much more rapid than fast tapping accompanied by repetition of the word 'fast'. The word does not exert a regulatory influence in the sense of bringing about behaviour which conforms to it. Indeed, the verbal performance simply interferes with the motor task. Repetition of the word 'slow' had the same effect. It slows down fast tapping but no more than does the repetition of 'fast'. The overt repetition of a word simply imposes a load on the nervous system regardless of its meaning. Fig. 1 gives the mean scores for 24 subjects. The effect was found for every single subject.

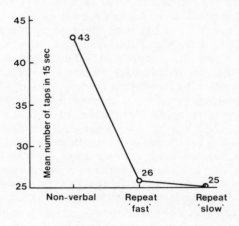

Fig. 1
Rate of fast tapping when accompanied by a repeated word

This experiment suggests two conclusions: (1) that the regulation observed by Meichenbaum and Goodman was at least in part an artefact of their experimental instructions, and (2) that the interference that they observed, used by Wozniak as indirect evidence in favour of Luria, can be analysed perfectly well without appeal to ideas remotely resembling the regulatory thesis. So far this is a small piece of evidence, but it is worth pursuing.

The significance of what is at stake needs stressing. The interference effects which Wozniak tries to use as indirect evidence for Luria's theories were not discovered in one isolated case. They were noted by Wilder (1969), Miller *et al.* (1970), Fletcher (1962), Birch (1971), by Wozniak himself, and of course by Meichenbaum and Goodman (1969), and by myself in the experiment above. Indeed the interference effect is one of the few observations which has achieved a wide basis of support from experimenters with quite different concerns, most of whom were not even looking for it.

If an experimental situation can be found where verbal inhibition of the motor system is a prominent and manipulable feature then it ought to be possible to shed more light on the crucial question: viz., is the interference observed in the American experiments of the kind that enters into Luria's conception of regulation, or is the hint provided by my tapping experiment, the more correct? The way to answer this question is to derive predictions from the differing analyses of the interference effects provided by the regulatory and capacity theories.

COMPARING REGULATORY AND CAPACITY ACCOUNTS OF INTERFERENCE

Recall Luria's typical experiment in which a child is presented with a sequence of red and blue light signals, but this time imagine that the child has to press a *blue* response button when a *red* light comes on, and vice versa. In other words he must switch his responses round from a natural or matching form to one which is 'incompatible' with the stimuli. If the child is of an age where his responses are supposed to be regulated by internal self-instructions then Luria's account would be like this: first, there will be a verbal analysis of the stimulus, 'is the light red or blue?' A covert label will be applied, say, 'red'. Then there will be the verbal organization of the motor act having the form of a self-instruction, perhaps, 'if see red press blue', or, 'red so blue'. On the basis of Vygotsky's work on the compression of inner speech this will become '. . . blue'. The stimulus label will become tacit (1962, pp. 100, 139, 145).

Suppose the task is made more complicated by asking the subject to produce an overt verbal output as well as the motor response. The subject will have to produce a word at the very same moment that he is alleged to be giving himself covert self-instructions. Furthermore he can be required to produce either the same word or the 'opposite' word to the one assumed to be controlling the motor output. If he is asked to say 'red' when he is alleged to be telling himself 'blue', then this should interfere with the motor task more than if he is required to say 'blue'. On the other hand if the capacity theory is true then both verbal outputs would interfere equally with the motor task.

This experimental situation is easy to produce and manipulate. Both the response modalities can be made compatible or incompatible with the stimuli and with each other. There are in fact four possibilities. These are given in Table 1.

Table 1

EXPERIMENTAL CONDITIONS

Condition	1		2		3		4	
Colour of Stimulus Light	Red	Blue	Red	Blue	Red	Blue	Red	Blue
Required button press	Red	Blue	Red	Blue	Blue	Red	Blue	Red
Required verbal response	Red	Blue	Blue	Red	Red	Blue	Blue	Red

In what has been called condition 1 everything matches, the stimulus, the button press and the spoken colour label. In condition 4, by contrast, the button to be pressed and the spoken word match or are compatible with one another, but both of them are opposite or incompatible with the stimuli.

The regulatory and capacity theories differ in their predictions about how subjects should perform in these two conditions. The crucial variable for Luria is whether the child is able to give himself proper self-instructions. In both of these cases the response modalities are compatible. There will be no attenuation or interference of the self-instruction. It must be granted that the condition where the responses are both opposite to the stimuli will be of somewhat greater difficulty, but in general the two should be roughly on a par. The key variable is the coordination of the verbal and motor systems. Other variables can be assumed to be negligibly small since they are given no prominence in Luria's analysis.

If the regulatory theory predicts that conditions 1 and 4 of Table 1 will be similar, the capacity theory leads to the expectation that they will be significantly different. Suppose that it takes a certain quantity of capacity, say x units, to label a light by its correct colour name. In order to give it the 'opposite' colour label certain acts of memory and transpositions are required which demand a further quantity of capacity, say x^1 units. On this theory the motor system works totally independently but according to exactly the same general principles. The corresponding capacity requirement for pressing a button of the same colour as the stimulus might be y units and the increment for the opposite button y^1 units. The total capacity required to perform the simple condition 1, will be $x + y$.

The capacity required to switch both responses round for condition 4 will be $x + y + x^1 + y^1$. There is no reason to assume that the increments required by S-R incompatibility are small, so the two conditions should differ significantly with the doubly incompatible condition the more difficult of the two.

I conducted an experiment with twenty-four seven-year olds. They were all given the same randomized sequence of ten red and ten blue light signals. Each signal lasted one second with two seconds between them. All subjects were given the four conditions of Table 1. The simple condition 1 was given first, and the other three in an order which was randomized across subjects. Finally the first condition was re-run. The average number of correct responses for the most simple and the doubly incompatible conditions are given in Table 2.

Table 2

MEAN NUMBER OF CORRECT RESPONSES OUT OF 20

Subjects	Motor responses		Verbal responses	
	condition 1	condition 4	condition 1	condition 4
Male	18	8	19	10
Female	19	13	20	13

(These differences are sig. at the $0 \cdot 01$ level on a two-tailed test)

The simple condition 1 produces a nearly perfect average performance. The doubly incompatible condition 4 drops down to an average around the 50% mark.

These results by no means prove that Luria's theory is wrong, because the experiment is seeking to compare rather indeterminate predictions. What it does show is that the two conditions *are* different and that the variable of S-R compatibility must be taken very seriously. To this extent the result favours the capacity theory.

Much more decisive predictions can be derived concerning those experimental conditions where the motor and verbal systems are incompatible with one another. Here the subject says 'red' when he has to press a blue button, and vice versa. (Notice that one or other of the response modalities must also be incompatible with the stimulus—see what are called conditions 2 and 3 of Table 1, p. 92).

According to the regulatory theory the verbal system is here working in opposition to the motor system. It is undermining the verbal instructions on which the motor responses depend. The motor system ought to be continuously making mistakes by following the overt verbal instructions which run counter to the correct covert ones. 'Opposite' motor responses should continuously intrude. The verbal system by contrast is conceived to be the more powerful and dominant partner and so it will be correspondingly free of intrusions. In short, where the verbal and motor systems are thrown into opposition the verbal system should dominate. Subjects should in general do what they say rather than say what they do.

The capacity theory makes quite different predictions. There is no question of the verbal system always imposing itself on the motor system. Errors of response will not be caused in the way that Luria imagines but solely by those factors which force either or both systems to exceed their respective capacity allocations. Verbal and motor tasks should both be performed correctly even if the verbal task involves an erroneous self-instruction—provided both tasks are within the capacity limitations of the subject. If one of the tasks is made more difficult it will begin to show errors once it oversteps the attention, memory and decision making resources allocated to it. This applies regardless of whether the increase in difficulty occurs in the motor or the verbal system.

In the present experiment the capacity theory predicts that errors will show in whichever response modality is incompatible with the stimulus situation. In particular the capacity and regulatory theory diverge in their predictions about what Table 1 calls condition 2. In this condition the motor system is compatible with the stimuli because the correct button to push is the same colour as the signal. The verbal responses are incompatible with the stimuli, and of course with the motor system. The subject must speak the 'wrong' colour label. Under these conditions the verbal system will be under pressure because it requires more capacity than if it were simply issuing correct responses. Mistakes are to be expected in the labelling, and these will characteristically derive from lapses back into compatibility. *It will thus appear that the motor system is dominating the verbal system and that the subject is saying what he does rather than doing what he says:* a result which is unthinkable on the regulatory model.

Of course, the capacity theory does not see the predicted distribution of errors as deriving from the domination of one system over another. The 'regulation' is only an appearance—a pseudo-regulation. The same applies to the other experimental condition where the verbal and motor systems are at odds (called condition 3 in Table 1). Here the capacity theory predicts the same as the regulatory theory. More mistakes should be found in the motor than in the verbal system. But again this will not derive from the verbal system imposing its pattern of response on the motor system. The regulation will be pseudo-regulation whose real cause is lapse back to less taxing compatible responses.

The experimental data falls into the form predicted by the capacity theory, as can be seen in Fig. 2.

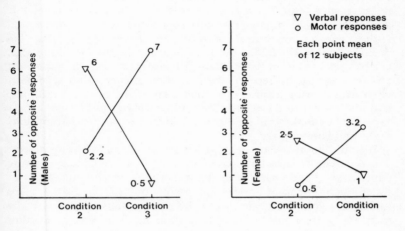

Fig. 2

The influence of S-R compatibility on the number of motor and verbal errors

Examination of this figure reveals that whichever response modality is incompatible with the stimuli shows the greater number of 'opposite' responses. Conversely the system which appears to dominate is the one which happens to be compatible with the stimuli. The graphs clearly reveal the predicted pseudo-regulation of the verbal system by the motor system.[1]

These experimental results have been introduced to shed light on the kind of interference that was consistently observed by the American experimenters. The decision about its nature was to be made on the basis of the success of the regulatory theory to make

1. When the male and female subjects are combined the differences between the number of motor and verbal errors in conditions 2 and 3 respectively are significant at the ·05 level using a two-tailed test. This result has been tested using two other groups of six-and-a-half-year olds with similar results.

predictions from its analysis of the phenomenon. The evidence indicates that the interference derives from capacity limitations imposed upon the otherwise independent verbal and motor systems. The interference phenomenon actually provides more evidence against the regulatory theory than it does for it.

In summary the situation is this. First, the defence of the regulatory theory against the failed replications is based on stressing the inhibition of perseveration as the central feature of that theory. This does not do justice to it. The regulatory theory also makes strong claims about the role of language in initiating responses. The attempted replications are therefore not off-target to the degree that the defence claims. The failure of the replications to find the results that can be predicted from the regulatory theory must count as important evidence against it. Second, the inhibition effects which have been cited as a possible source of explanation of the negative findings, and also as indirect evidence for Luria's theory, in fact seem best explained by making quite different, indeed opposite, assumptions to the regulatory theory.

It would be unfair to end without stressing the following points. The regulatory theory has proved itself highly valuable in suggesting experiments, and there is no reason why it should not yield an indefinite number of interesting predictions in the future. This makes it a good scientific theory. Moreover, the situation is really more fluid than my account may have made it sound. Further experiments may change the balance of power. But over and above this I would submit that the prominence of interference effects shows that they deserve at least as much attention as the alleged phenomenon of verbal regulation—and the crucial concept for studying interference is surely that of limited channel capacity.[1]

1. The capacity theory as it is presented here is in need of considerable refinement. For example, another factor needs to be introduced to allow for R-R incompatibility as well as S-R compatibility. This is a step in the direction of Luria's theory but still falls far short of any assumption to the effect that the verbal system controls the pattern of responses of the motor system. Another feature of the theory that needs investigating is the influence of the subject's strategies for differentially allocating capacity on the basis of the perceived importance of the verbal and motor tasks. Both of these points along with other complexities and difficulties in the theory are discussed in my *Speech and the Regulation of Behaviour* (Bloor, 1971). For an extension of the theory into adult behaviour in self-paced tasks see Bloor (1972), where an attempt has been made to allocate numerical values to the theoretical parameters.

Birch, D. (1971). Evidence for competition and coordination between vocal and manual responses in preschool children. *Journal of Experimental Child Psychology*, 12 (1), 10-26. (Quote by Wozniak, 1972.)

Bloor, D. (1971). *Speech and the regulation of behaviour*. Unpublished Ph.D. thesis, University of Edinburgh.

Bloor, D. (1972). Commands and countermands in a card sorting task. Unpublished report. Duplicated copies from the Science Studies Unit, University of Edinburgh.

Broadbent, D. (1958). *Perception and communication*. Oxford: Pergamon.

Fletcher, S. G. (1962). Speech as an element in the organisation of a motor response. *Journal of Speech and Hearing Research*, 5 (3), 292-300.

Jarvis, P. E. (1963). *The effect of self-administered verbal instructions on simple sensory-motor performance in children*. Unpublished Ph.D. thesis, University of Rochester, New York.

Joynt, D. and Cambourne, D. (1968). Psycholinguistic development and the control of behaviour. *British Journal of Educational Psychology*, 38, 249-60.

Luria, A. R. (1932). *The nature of human conflicts*. Trans. Gantt, W. Horsley, New York: Liveright.

Luria, A. R. (1961). *The role of speech in the regulation of normal and abnormal behaviour*. Ed. Tizard, J.: Oxford: Pergamon.

Meichenbaum, D. and Goodman, J. (1969). The developmental control of operant motor responding by verbal operants. *Journal of Experimental Child Psychology*, 7, 553-65.

Miller, S., Shelton, J. and Flavell, J. (1970). A test of Luria's hypothesis concerning the development of verbal self-regulation. *Child Development*, 41, 651-65.

Vygotsky, L. S. (1962). *Thought and language*. Ed. and trans. Hanfmann, E. and Vakar, G., Cambridge, Mass., MIT Press.

Wilder, L. (1969). The role of speech and other extra-signal feedback in the regulation of the child's sensory motor behaviour. *Speech Monographs*, 36, 425-34.

Wozniak, R. H. (1972). Verbal regulation of motor behaviour—Soviet research and non-Soviet replications. *Human Development*, 15, 13-57.

Note: I have cited works only where they relate to the particular controversy that I have tried to analyse. Access to the large body of material bearing upon Luria's theory can be gained by consulting the bibliographies of the above papers in conjunction with the valuable surveys in O'Connor, N. (Ed.), *Present Day Russian Psychology*, Oxford: Pergamon, 1966. The work on retarded children which bears on the Russian theory is also extensive. This territory can be approached via O'Connor, N. and Hermelin, B., Cognitive defects in children, *British Medical Bulletin*, 27 (3), 1971.

The Silence of Stupidity

JOANNA RYAN
Formerly Senior Assistant in Research, Unit for Research into Medical Applications in Psychology, University of Cambridge

CONTENTS

ON INVESTIGATING SUBNORMALITY

Until the last decade the language skills of those classified as 'subnormal'[1] have not been much investigated. Language studies of various kinds are now however becoming increasingly popular, a fashion that is probably a spin off from the general increase of psychological interest in language and language acquisition. The psychological study of mental subnormality has not tended to give rise autonomously to questions and theories of its own, but rather has tended to take issues and ideas from other fields of psychological inquiry and apply them to subnormals without much thought as to whether they are relevant to the lives of such people. Nevertheless there are some specific reasons why language should be a central concern in the study and education of the subnormal, as of people generally. Conceptions of human nature have over the past century increasingly emphasized the language-using, rule-following and symbol-generating capacities of human beings, as contrasted with animals. Moral and spiritual qualities receive much less emphasis than they used to as a distinguishing feature of human nature. Generalized and implicit conceptions of human nature often pre-determine the kinds of questions that are asked in psychology, and the theoretical terms with which we describe people. The study of stupidity is often very revealing in this respect since many severely subnormal people stretch our notions of what it is to be human, and blur the distinctions between human and sub-human existence. The language we use about them is indicative of this: 'vegetative' is often used as a descriptive term for the severest degrees of subnormality, and 'animal'—or even unfit for animals—for the conditions in some of the worst hospitals.

Stratification by intelligence both reflects and reinforces particular values in our society, but it is verbal intelligence that is especially

1. A note on terminology: the descriptive categories used in this area change frequently in the useless quest for stigma-free labels. Here idiocy, stupidity, mental deficiency, mental subnormality and mental retardation are used as the context merits. The more euphemistic terms, such as exceptionality, are avoided.

important. 'General' tests of intelligence are primarily verbal tests in what they measure. They also involve understanding and compliance with verbal instructions, and verbal skills in answering. The division between mental and manual labour has a strong class basis, and is reflected in the much greater value attached to verbal as opposed to non-verbal or performance intelligence. Minorities and out-groups of all kinds, and the working class as a whole, are increasingly seen in terms of deficiencies in verbal intelligence and linguistic skills. These supposed deficiencies are the main targets of contemporary Headstart and other compensatory education programs involving ethnic minorities, working class 'deprived' and other social 'subnormals' in the USA and Britain. Educational failure, if it is not seen in terms of low IQ, tends to be 'explained' in terms of linguistic and related deviations from middle class norms. In the psychological and educational literature the verbal deficiencies of subnormals are often emphasized, and occupational training is almost exclusively for tasks that do not involve the exercise of any verbal skills at all—usually the simplest manual ones.

Before reviewing some of the research that has been done on the language abilities of subnormals (pp. 105-22), it is necessary to explain the ways in which subnormals have been described and categorized, the methods used to investigate their behaviour, and the kinds of research questions asked. Such a background is essential for interpreting the research 'findings'. It can only be presented very briefly here: more detailed accounts will be found in Ryan 1973a, 1973b and 1976.

Before the advent of intelligence tests (c. 1908) and the idea of a continuum of intelligence, idiocy tended to be seen as a matter of kind—either you were an idiot without a mind (ament) or you had one and were normal. The notion of degrees of idiocy only came to dominate the field, as it does today, with the advent of the technology of testing. Most of the nineteenth century classifications that were suggested concerned symptomology, syndrome analysis, and speculative causation (e.g. cretinism, Down's syndrome or mongolism). Esquirol (1772-1840), a French doctor, was one of the few people to propose a classification by degree and interestingly enough the criteria were verbal ones: imbeciles were those who could communicate verbally, and idiots were divided into three classes, those who could use words and short sentences, those who only used monosyllables and grunts, and those with no speech at all. Howe, an American doctor who was responsible for spreading many European ideas about the care of idiots to America in the mid nineteenth century, proposed a similar classification by degree on the basis of the capacity of using language as 'signs of thought'. This was part of an argument for the notion that idiots were not people without minds (all or none conception), but people with feeble minds. Early educational influences were not however much concerned with language, but tended to concentrate on sensory training, and also, particularly in the large public institutions, on motor skills that would be useful occupationally. Even after the advent of IQ tests, and the setting up of 'special' schools within the educational system, sensory, motor and social skills took precedence over verbal ones.

It is only since the late 1960s, with the outside influence from linguistics and psychology generally, and from compensatory education, that language programs have been initiated in subnormal schools, and the importance of language in general development emphasized to future teachers. Along with this there has been a great increase in the amount of 'pure' research on the language abilities of the subnormal and also in 'applied' research on how to improve them verbally. In Russia (where the study of stupidity is unblushingly called defectology) there has been a much more consistent interest in language skills, and research seems to have been much more closely tied to pedagogic needs (see Segal, 1966, for a useful review). Russian conceptualizations of the development of language, particularly the distinction between motor and verbal systems, have influenced some pure research in the West (e.g. O'Connor and Hermelin, 1963) but have not led to the kind of training programs that Russian special schools employ; instead most English and American programs tend to be influenced by either Chomskian notions of grammar, or by Skinnerian methods, or by some pragmatic combination of both (see McLean, Yoder and Schiefelbusch, 1972). Thus we get grammatical training, using Chomskian descriptive methods, taught piecemeal with reinforcement on an operant design.

Before the advent of psychological theories, poverty of speech and language was seen in what is perhaps still a common-sense way—namely as reflecting poverty of thought and reason. The idiot has no ideas to express, no propositions to formulate. It is only ideas and propositions that need any elaborate language, since basic needs can be expressed by grunts, monosyllables or gestures. On this view there would be no point in trying to teach language skills since there are no thoughts present to be expressed. Modern psychology has departed considerably from this position in a variety of ways.

Firstly, language skills have been described and studied in relative isolation from their social and cognitive use. Modern psycholinguistics has greatly contributed to this emphasis, which in terms of volume of research has dominated the field. Much of this work consists in descriptive comparisons of subnormal and 'normal' groups with reference to specific verbal skills, especially grammatical ones (see the next section).

Secondly, the question of the relations between language and thought has been associated with the idea that whatever the quality or quantity of subnormal thought, there is also an additional difficulty in the verbal expression of such thoughts. Subnormals do not use language to think with and, the implication goes, their thought is the worse for it. Different psychologists have put forward different ideas as to why the subnormal tend not to think verbally (assuming this is true)—basically meditation versus production deficiency positions. It is not intended to review this kind of research here, mainly because the categories used (language as against thought, verbal as against non-verbal thought or encoding etc.) are, to the present author, a mystification, and incapable of any consistent and meaningful empirical application. Interested readers are referred to Morris (1975) for a consideration of how to distinguish between verbal and non-verbal encoders, and of the lack of consistency in findings in this area, and also to Bryant (1970) for a general review of the theoretical issues.

The traditional attitude within mental subnormality research towards the psycholinguistic skills of subnormals has been the 'defect' position, as it has been the main mode of approach in non-language aspects of behaviour. This approach is basically comparative and descriptive, aiming to identify particular defects in subnormal performance apart from the overall slowness of development. The general strategy of investigation is to select two groups of subjects matched for general stage of development but differing in IQ and compare them on some specific task or treatment. The most usual basis for matching two groups is mental age or chronological age though sometimes more task specific criteria are used. Such methods of investigation have been criticized on grounds of the validity of comparing subnormal development with 'normal' development at all, and particularly using the matching methods usually employed (see Ryan, 1973a and b). Apart from the issue of the adequacy of the experimental controls and variables selected for matching, there is also the more basic question of whether any comparisons of a subnormal with a 'normal' person's abilities are valid in these terms given the totally different life experiences involved (see the next section for a consideration of this). Another criticism of this research methodology is that it assumes without question the possibility of generalizing about the subnormal population as a whole and does not sufficiently take into account the extensive variability that exists, and that is intrinsic to the nature of subnormality. Mental subnormality has a very large number of different causes, and conditions associated with it, and in addition the majority of cases do not have any firm diagnosis of cause. As well as the diversity of causes, the consequences of being subnormal in terms of family life and social and educational experiences are likely to differ widely amongst subnormal people, through various extremes. Any one experimental group is likely to be heterogeneous with respect to diagnostic group and life history, and to differ from any other experimental group in the nature of this heterogeneity in a way that is usually left unspecified in most research. This uncontrolled variability in the subject population probably accounts for the relative failure to find empirical 'laws' characterizing subnormal behaviour, despite extensive efforts.

The theoretical posing of research questions in terms of supposed defects of subnormals—whether defects in language, memory, attention, reaction times or whatever—has been associated with a preoccupation with organic pathology, and the presumed causation of behavioural defects by such pathological brain mechanisms. The absence of any concrete and specific neurological knowledge has not stopped psychologists inventing hypothetical brain mechanisms, such as 'inadequate stimulus trace strength' or 'weakness in the second signalling system'. This has led to the location of all alleged defects in the heads of subnormals—or rather, in the hole in their heads. It has prevented us from understanding their behaviour in any environmental and social terms at all. The absence of any studies about how we as 'normal' adults behave to subnormal people is very striking. One aim of this section is to present an alternative approach in this respect.

In what follows, work that does have these general methodological deficiencies will necessarily be referred to but these strictures should not be forgotten. They apply to the author's own empirical study as well as to that of others.

SUBNORMALITY WITH LANGUAGE

This section is concerned with subnormal people (mostly children) who do acquire some degree of language skill, the next section with those who have not acquired language or who acquire it only as a result of extensive intervention programs.

One of the main questions asked has been whether subnormal children have a greater difficulty with language compared to other areas of development and relative to 'normal' development. For reasons indicated above this is an unsatisfactory question that cannot be answered in any precise or non-circular way. It is only in the case of radical unevenness in development that we can easily identify language 'defects' and in these cases there is no need of dubious comparison methods, e.g. with autistic or so called non-communicating children there is no doubt that language is an area of major backwardness. Here studies that compare different groups of subnormal children and that attempt to relate differences in rate of language development either to environmental differences or to diagnostic ones will be considered. Then possible differences between subnormal and 'normal' children in the processes of language acquisition, as opposed to differences in the relative rates of development, will be discussed in relation to what scattered evidence there is and to speculations about developmental processes.

Some of the ideas below have evolved in the course of a study carried out by the author on the language development of severely subnormal children. This will be briefly described here as it will be referred to on several occasions. Three groups of children, one of mean IQ of 103 and mean age of 2 years 11 months, two of mean IQ of 40 and aged between 5 and 9 were used. The two subnormal groups differed as regards etiology, one consisting only of known Down's syndrome children (mongols), the other being of mixed and varied etiology. The groups were matched for mean mental age (Stanford-Binet) of 3 years 1 month and approximate matching was obtained for social class of parents, sex composition of the groups, and living situation (at home). All children attended either school (old junior training centres) or nursery school or crèches daily. Each child was seen five or six times over a period of two weeks. Extensive recordings were made of their speech during play with the experimenter, and these were transcribed and analysed. A variety of verbal and other tests were administered. The tests included noun vocabulary (pictures and objects), preposition comprehension, grammatical comprehension, verbal short-term memory for sentences, non-verbal (visual) memory. The children were seen again to assess developmental changes. The subnormal children were tested after a gap of fourteen months, the 'normal' children after $3\frac{1}{2}$ months, the rationale of this being roughly equivalent developmental time.

Comparisons between groups of subnormal children
Comparisons between different etiological groups are often unsatisfactory both because of diagnostic ignorance in the majority of cases, and because of the large number of known different conditions and causes of mental subnormality. This means that the numbers in most known categories are very small indeed. These difficulties do not however mean that etiological variation can be neglected as it has been in most psychological research. Mongols, because of their relatively easy diagnosis and frequency, have been

the subgroup most investigated. It should be noted that the implicit comparison group of remaining non-mongol subnormals will vary just as much (or more) from study to study, and so mongols are not being compared with a known or equivalent population in all or even any studies. This limits the validity of reported findings, and indeed may be the explanation for lack of consistency in some findings.

It is commonly held that mongols are relatively inferior with respect to verbal skills compared to other subnormals. The evidence is fairly consistent in suggesting a higher incidence of articulatory and voice disorders amongst mongols (Evans and Hampson, 1968, provide a detailed review of this) but it is much less consistent with respect to grammatical and semantic aspects of language. Lyle (1960) found mongols to be inferior to other subnormals matched for non-verbal mental age as regards word definition tasks and grammatical complexity of spontaneous speech, but equal as regards one-word vocabulary tests. Mongol children were more vulnerable than the others to the adverse effects of institution living on their language development. Mein (1961) found mongols to be slower than other subnormals in their vocabulary development. However Evans and Hampson (1968), in their review of mongol language abilities, conclude that there is no particular and consistent association between mongolism and language difficulty other than in phonological skills. Belmont (1971) in an extensive review of medico-behavioural research in subnormality, and of mongolism in particular, does not even mention possible language deficiencies though he does suggest difficulty with auditory encoding. My own study failed to find any large differences between the mongol and the other subnormal group, whereas there were large differences between the subnormal and 'normal' group. There were however many non-significant differences, all in the direction of relative mongol inferiority, on measures of grammatical complexity and verbal memory, but not on vocabulary scores. These findings are similar in direction to Lyle's mentioned above. In the developmental comparisons over time the non-mongol group showed a non-significant improvement in mean utterance length scores whereas the mongol group did not show any change at all.

One factor of considerable importance in considering these suggestions about mongol verbal abilities is the high incidence of mild hearing impairments, evidence for which is now considerable (e.g. Fulton and Lloyd, 1968). These hearing impairments are often caused by, or related to, malformations in the respiratory passage and associated structures, and the high chance of various respiratory infections. Such respiratory and auditory difficulties are sufficient to account for the results which have indicated mongol inferiority as regards language. Buddenhagen's (1971) detailed account provides vivid evidence of how speech training was impossible during periods of nasal congestion—a condition mongols are particularly prone to and that is more likely to obtain under conditions of mass child care, as in institutions. Buddenhagen also provides a compelling account of how such physiological defects if responded to negatively by those responsible for the child, can result in total mutism and categorization as a non-speaker, when in a better environment with more attention to nose wiping as well as to control of infection etc. the child would have been perfectly able to acquire language. This is a good example of the interaction of the biological and the social. The point should also be made that different 'aspects of language' cannot be considered to be independent, as is sometimes suggested by the way they are studied. Difficulties with phonology, for physiological reasons, may lead to difficulties with grammar and semantics, for essentially social reasons.

Comparisons of children living in institutions with those living at home show the expected results that those living in institutions, especially large ones, are much slower in their language development (Lyle, 1960). Many studies have emphasized how unsuited large hospitals are to language acquisition (e.g. King, Raynes and Tizard, 1971). Case studies sometimes show regression in verbal abilities after admission to hospital.

In the present study no differences were found between subnormal children from different social class homes, whereas the usual differences (middle class superiority) were found within the 'normal' group. Absence of the usual social class correlations with subnormal children has also been reported in another study not concerned with language but with general early development (Carr, 1970). Possible reasons for this are suggested below.

Language acquisition

Apart from questions about relative developmental rate, psychologists have also been concerned with the way in which subnormal children acquire language. Such qualitative questions avoid some of the pitfalls of the more quantitative ones, but there are still some basic methodological problems about matching and control, and about what is considered 'normal'. It is usually assumed, especially in advice to teachers, that both the course of language development, and also the processes involved in its acquisition are essentially similar in normal and subnormal children, simply much slower in the latter. There is in fact considerable evidence supporting this former idea as far as syntax, morphology, and semantics goes.

Lenneberg, Nicholas and Rosenberger (1964) found that mongol children passed through all the same 'stages' in the usual order. Lackner (1968) in a very detailed study of grammatical rules in five severely subnormal children, found no basic differences from what he assumed 'normal' development to be. Graham and Graham (1971) came to the same conclusions. Analysis of 'spontaneous' speech records in the present study showed the same variety and range of various constructions (e.g. 'complete' sentences, incomplete ones of various kinds, verb transformations, 'ready-mades') in subnormal and normal children when selected and matched for mean utterance length of their speech. Subnormal children were also found to make the same kinds of errors of omission, substitution and over-generalization of syntactical items as did the 'normal' children. Lenneberg et al. (1964) also noticed that the grammatical errors that subnormal children made were essentially common errors of the kind that have been much vaunted as showing the rule-following nature of children's language skills. Studies using the Berko morphology tests also show the usual patterns of error (e.g. Dever and Gardner, 1970). As regards semantics and associated topics, a variety of studies report no qualitative differences e.g. Semmel et al. (1968) for word associations, Beier, Startweather and Lambert (1969) for vocabulary counts, O'Connor and Hermelin (1963) for semantic generalization.

It can be concluded that subnormal children considered as a whole group do not show any peculiarities in the organization of their grammatical and semantic knowledge—*what* they are learning and the errors they make in learning it, are much the same as 'normal' children, in as far as generalization is possible in either case. One might indeed query the likelihood of any other result having been found, given that the children are acquiring any language at all, and given how basic some of the features investigated are to the nature and structure of language. A consideration of the more salient differences in other respects will put the similarities in some kind of perspective.

Large differences in the frequency of various kinds of articulation and voice disorders are usually recorded. The estimates of course vary greatly between studies (see Spradlin, 1963; Jordan, 1967, for reviews). In general the incidence is much greater in institutionalized subnormals than in those living at home, but even in the latter group there is a raised incidence in several respects compared to normal children. Lyle (1961) found the discrimination and reproduction of speech sounds to be inferior in a group of home-living subnormal children matched for non-verbal mental age with a group of higher IQ. In my present study, the effective intelligibility for transcribing purposes was much lower in the subnormal groups than in the comparison groups even when those with equal mean utterance lengths were compared.

Although there is very little evidence about the specific kinds of speech sound difficulties that do occur, some suggestions may be advanced as to their possible causation. Some may be related to the high incidence of both major and minor neurological impairments found in most groups of subnormal children. For example, Birch *et al.* (1967) found that half of an unselected sample of high grade ESN children had some kind of CNS impairment. The proportion is likely to be even higher in lower grade groups. In the present study a modified version of Garfield *et al.*'s (1966) motor impersistence tests showed very large differences between 'normal' and subnormal groups. The additional possibility of uncorrected defective hearing has already been mentioned above in connection with mongol children, and Lloyd and Fulton (1972) emphasize the generally raised incidence of hearing impairments in all subnormal people. The role of adults in the child's environment in maintaining defective articulation has not been investigated—but for various reasons, either lack of attention, or acceptance of partial intelligibility and a reluctance to correct it, is probably important.

Another kind of difference between subnormal and 'normal' language acquisition concerns differential patterning and difficult intercorrelations between various verbal skills. Both Lyle's (1961) study and the present author's, showed that the subnormal children were equal to, or in some cases better than, the 'normal' comparison groups on extensive noun vocabulary tests involving both recognition and naming. In both studies this similarity with respect to level of single word vocabulary development was accompanied by subnormal inferiority with respect to many aspects of grammatical and phonological skills. In the present study scores on all the different verbal tests and speech measures were intercorrelated in a matrix. The 'normal' group showed a much greater number of significant intercorrelations than either of the two subnormal groups. This implies that there is much more consistency within the 'normal' group as regards the relative difficulty of the various tests than in the subnormal group who were much more heterogeneous. For any one subnormal child his or her score on any one test is much less predictable from his or her performance on other tests than is the case for a 'normal' child. Such variability in other areas of behaviour has also been found for subnormals, both between and within individuals, e.g. reaction time scores (Baumeister, 1968). It is likely that the slowness of subnormal development is associated with rather uneven and piecemeal development. In terms of a 'stage' view of development, it has been suggested by Inhelder (1943) that some deficient children get stuck or fixated at particular stages for undue lengths of time. Inhelder in fact described their development in terms of unstable 'oscillations', meaning great variability in actual performance, associated with superficial acquisition of particular schema. This unstable oscillation was apparently combined with greater difficulty than in 'normal' children in progressing from one stage to the next. This description is rather similar to the combination of variability mentioned above with the rigidity previously described by others (e.g. Kounin, 1941). Piecemeal development i.e. learning of specific skills with inability to generalize to others, will lead to a much less integrated set of skills compared to 'normal' children, and therefore a lack of consolidation of schemas characteristic of Piagetian 'stages'. Difficulty in generalizing spontaneously has also been shown in transfer of learning experiments (Clarke and Clarke, 1967).

The developmental comparisons in the present study are relevant here. It was found that over a period of roughly fourteen months the subnormal children as a group did not show any significant improvement in various grammatical measures both from spontaneous speech recordings and from more formal tests. Some children got worse. The 'normal' comparison group showed significant improvement in the same measures during a hypothetically equivalent 'mental age time' of $3\frac{1}{2}$ months. By contrast both groups, subnormal and 'normal', did show an equal improvement in the single word vocabulary scores. Thus although many of the subnormal children were static in some aspects of their development, they were changing in other aspects.

These last considerations raise the possibility that the processes of language acquisition may be importantly altered in subnormal children, even if the overall course of it is roughly 'normal'. In what follows some suggestions will be made about the kind of multiple interactions of different processes—or their absence—that are relevant to subnormal children, or at least to some of them.

Cunningham (1974) states, with some evidence, that subnormal children show less exploratory behaviour and fewer spontaneous learning activities than do 'normal' children. As infants they are also found to be more passive in response to sensory and other stimulation. One implication of this is that subnormal children are not only less likely to learn anything from any given environment but are also less likely to produce new learning environments for themselves. This lower probability of self-produced learning environments will apply to human interaction too. Subnormal children will be less likely to create a facilitative human environment for themselves if they behave in a way that makes it difficult for adults to respond to them, either at all, or in a way that is extending or instructive. The various ways in which a subnormal child may be a poor stimulus for and/or reinforcer of, particular kinds of parental and adult behaviour are complex and at present scarcely investigated. However a few suggestions can be made.

'Expectations' cover a wide range of phenomena. At a general level there is a strong cultural tendency to judge people by how they talk. With children one common criterion of brightness is how well they talk. Stupid people may 'pass' as normal until they open their mouths, as Edgerton (1967) has recorded. Such general cultural assumptions may lead people, including subnormal people, to expect that subnormal people will speak badly and understand little. At the moment we have only rather unsatisfactory evidence about the effects of expectations on measured ability but a generalized expectancy effect as regards incompetence spread over a child's lifetime is easy to believe in. It has frequently been demonstrated in other areas (e.g. industrial training, use of behaviour modification) that we have much too low expectations about the final levels of performance that can be achieved by subnormal individuals, given suitable methods and time. Specifically as regards language one way in which low expectations may work is that they may lead others to talk too simply to subnormal individuals, and thus not provide them with a verbal environment from which they can learn. Edgerton's (1967) documentation of the lives of mentally retarded people released from hospital, describes how they feel that 'normal' people talk down to them, by talking too loudly, with exaggerated slowness and emphasis, and as though the recipient will not understand. In general much more work needs to be done on how we behave towards those categorized as stupid, and how their behaviour can be related to our behaviour, and ours to theirs. In education particularly the concern has been so exclusively with 'helping' the child that the behaviour of teachers towards subnormal children has not been investigated, particularly not the possibility that much of their behaviour and their roles within segregated schools may in fact be confirming the child in his or her stupid behaviour rather than alleviating it (Cooper, 1976).

There is increasing evidence suggesting that mothers of 'normal' children adjust their speech in accordance with the age and advancement of their children's verbal abilities (see Ryan, 1974a), but the exact way in which this is done in relation to the children's growing competence is not really clear. However there are some indications that with subnormal children this normally useful process may be taken to disadvantageous lengths. Spradlin and Rosenberg (1964) have shown empirically how adults change their speech according to the known IQ of subjects in an experiment, to the extent of talking in what they consider to be a linguistically unhelpful way with the lowest IQ groups, e.g. asking yes/no questions excessively. There is also a suggestion in Jeffree and Cashdan's work (1971) that parents tend to talk to their subnormal children in a way that only requires single word answers—often the names of objects. Casual observation in many subnormal schools suggests this may happen fairly often, even under the guise of stimulating language.

There are other ways in which parental behaviour may be discouraging rather than encouraging linguistically. For example the kind of idiosyncratic juxtapositions or omissions or over-generalizations that are considered 'intelligent' and creative errors when they occur in a bright middle class child may be devalued as ignorant or babyish and be heavily corrected when they occur in a subnormal child. The line between affirming and confirming a child in his or her attempts to communicate and on the other hand encouraging babyisms and incorrect speech is probably a difficult one for most mothers to draw. It is likely to be a much harder task with a slowly developing child, where developmental change is much less obvious to the mother, and there is much more anxiety about the child's competence.

There may also be other reasons apart from low expectations why, in as much as they do, adults talk over-simply to subnormal children. It may be that, whatever the individual's expectation concerning the child, it is much more difficult for a parent with a subnormal child to keep up the kind of rich verbal interpretation and extension of the child's utterance that has been described by Roger Brown and others. The functions of this expanding interpretative process are probably many (see Ryan, 1974, for a consideration of this), and there is no very clear cut evidence concerning its causal association with rate of development. However, it is plausible that such automatic responses on the part of adults towards developing children are extremely important aspects of how a child learns language, not just in terms of grammatical competence, but also in terms of the communicative and other social skills involved in language. Fenn (1973) has shown the efficacy of carefully planned grammatical and semantic expansion in improving severely subnormal institutionalized children's speech. The fact that these methods work in a training context does not of course imply that this is what happens at home, but the further fact that mothers (at least the white middle class mothers of advanced children studied by psychologists) do this extensively makes it likely. We do not at present know much about what maintains a mother's behaviour in terms of the child's responses, although we do know there is great individual variation, not obviously related to how advanced the child is linguistically (Brown, Cazden and Bellugi, 1969). This hypothesized greater difficulty in maintaining expansive and interpretative dialogues with a subnormal child would be different from, but of course interact with, the effects of low expectations mentioned above—in certain cases they could contribute to the same behaviour, or same absence of behaviour.

There is no observational data known to the writer of mothers' behaviour in a 'natural' situation that lends itself to testing this suggestion. One study (Marshall, *et al.*, 1973) that looked at mothers' behaviour in an experimental situation unfortunately compared subnormal children with 'normal' children of equal chronological age, so that the results are most readily interpretable in terms of the large mental age difference. They found that the subnormal children spoke less, but their mothers spoke more, than was the case with the comparison 'normal' group. They found that mothers of subnormal children addressed more mands (commands, requests etc.) to them in proportion to other types of speech categories than did mothers of 'normal' children. In the present author's study, there was no difference in the amount that the groups of subnormal children and 'normal' children of equivalent mental age spoke in 'free' play situations, as far as group averages went. Individual subnormal children however showed extremes of talkativeness and silence, not observed in the 'normal' group.

Possible reasons why it is harder for a mother of a subnormal child to initiate and maintain a verbally informative dialogue with her child are as follows. Firstly because of the child's slow development it is likely that she has heard the same utterance from the child many times before; she may be bored by what the child has said and by the highly predictable exchange that may ensue. Thus the lower probability of developmental change may in itself further lower the probability of future change. Secondly it is possible that within any one dialogue subnormal children tend to be more repetitive of themselves. Analysis of dialogue with a relatively strange adult in the present study suggested that extreme repetitiveness characterized some of the subnormal children's speech. Self-repetition is however often observed in young 'normal' children; its functions are hardly clear. The same is true of imitation of others—a few subnormal children show what are experienced as excessive amounts of imitation from the point of view of trying to maintain a conversation with them, but many are no more imitative than many young 'normal' children. Repeated insistent questioning with little regard to the answer is also found in some subnormal children. Self-repetition, imitation, routinized question-ing are all forms of speech that make it extremely hard for the 'other' to sustain related talk; for the adult at least (not necessarily for children) mutual reciprocated dialogue becomes impossible. We do not know to what extent such dialogue-inhibiting forms of utter-ance really do characterize most or even some subnormal children. The problem here is partly that these forms of conversation or non-conversation are probably highly functional at certain stages of language development (imitation certainly is) but become disadvan-tageous if they persist or predominate. Mothers respond selectively to different forms of utterance from their child (e.g. imitations as against 'spontaneous' words) in a way that probably discourages the former and encourages the latter, at least after a certain age. They are more likely to respond to, and expand, a spontaneous utterance than an imitation (Ryan, 1973c). It may be that mothers of sub-normal children lose some of this selectivity faced with scarcely changing behaviour over years, welcoming *any* form of speech rather than none, however unproductive conversationally. This may give rise to the persistence of some forms of speech.

One possible explanation for the absence of the usual social class correlations with language development (mentioned above) now becomes apparent. It is a very plausible supposition (again unproven since no really equivalent studies have been done with working class parents) that extensive and interpretative verbal dialogue is a salient middle class characteristic, along with the greater valuation of all verbal skills. This may well account for the 'normal' middle class superiority in language development. 'Normal' middle class parental behaviour may be more radically disrupted by a subnormal child, than that of a working class parent, because of the kind of behaviour involved, so that the usual advantage does not obtain.

Jeffree (1974) suggests a further kind of reason for the possible distortion of a subnormal child's language development. At the age when words are first produced the 'normal' child is still in frequent physical contact with the mother, with much picking up on her part, and face to face interaction of various kinds. This is also a time of particularly intensive attachment on the child's part. With an older, larger and often physically more advanced subnormal child, such physical contact and the associated kinds of interaction are less likely to occur at a time when the child is starting to talk. This in itself may further retard the child's development since there will be fewer use-ful opportunities for the extensive verbal, semi-verbal and non-verbal dialogues and interchanges carried on with a 'normal' child.

Mannoni (1964) presents a view of parent-child relationships with deficient children, and of the roles of doctors and educators, that is very relevant to the foregoing considerations. Her work, however, seems to have been completely ignored by those concerned with subnormal children, possibly because it has only recently been translated (1972), possibly because of her psychoanalytic theory, possibly because of the challenge her views present to established practices and roles. She combines a fairly complex view of early childhood—Lacan's development of Freudian theory—with a strong political critique of existing institutions and labelling practices. She presents a detailed account of how the anxieties of parents, doctors, and educators, concerning the deficient child, interact with each other, against what she considers the child's best interests. Using a large series of case histories from her clinical practice, she considers what the birth of a deficient child means to the mother, and within the whole family. For many mothers a deficient child is the death of various fantasies about how a child can fulfill certain expectations relating to her own past history and present marital relationships; in other cases the child is the focus of family sagas of illness and accidents. In some families the mother's relationship with the deficient child involves a gross degree of passivity and dependence on the child's part, and the virtual exclusion of the father. A contradictory state may arise where the mother both behaves as if she wishes the child could be cured or improved, but also is unable to give up the child's dependence on herself. Her anxieties, and those of others, are channelled into an excessive concern for education and remediation, which may well turn out to be useless, not because the child is intrinsically ineducable but because he or she has been irrevocably labelled as deficient and because a whole web of emotional relationships has been created around this 'fact' and these will not be changed by re-education of the child.

Mannoni is thus concerned to show how in studying or treating stupid children we see only the child's defect and not our own involvement—a point that has been put above, somewhat differently. She however develops this theme further namely that 'To wish to treat the symptom is to reject the child himself'. Rejecting the child means in her terms not cruel or negligent practices, but the denial of the child as an autonomous and desiring being in his or her own right. This leaves the child in a state of object. The precise means of 'object' and 'desire' depend on an acceptance of Lacan's extremely complex theorizing, but what is relevant in this context is that rejection of the child may lead to an incapacity to utilize the whole symbolic mode of relationship (and this for Mannoni is also related to the effective absence of fathers in many families). Whilst 'symbolic' has a much wider sense than just language abilities there is also an integral connection. A child whose development has been restricted in this way may not be able to express his or her desires, find out who he or she is. The simplest hypothesis that would 'explain' why (some) subnormal children have difficulty with verbal skills is that adults do not listen to them. Listening for Mannoni is the least that a psychotherapist can do for such children, and probably also the most that she can do, given the need that parents and others have for the rehabilitation and adjustment of the child. Essentially she sees 'special' education and other treatments as doing more for the adults involved in allaying their anxieties than it is likely to do for the child, who has received a verdict (label) from society against which he or she cannot appeal.

In this section it has been argued that the language skills of subnormal people cannot be considered in isolation from their social situations and life experiences. It has been emphasized how people's expectations of children labelled as subnormal may determine both the children's and the adults' behaviour. The ideas advanced essentially involve a consideration of the highly complex interactive nature of child development, of the values given to intelligence in our society, and of the effects of being categorized as deficient in this respect. The simplistic postulation of a 'language defect' does not do justice to the complexity of processes involved, nor to the range determinants of any one individual's behaviour.

SUBNORMALITY WITHOUT SPEECH

Apart from possible relative handicap with language and differences in acquisition processes, there are also many subnormal people who have passed the age of puberty without learning to speak, and who probably never will do so in the 'normal' course of their abnormal lives. Our ignorance about these people is very great. They, along with the physically handicapped, are the least investigated of all the mentally subnormal, and also the most vulnerable to present conditions of mass care. It is not possible to find any meaningful prevalence figures for non-speaking subnormals, partly because very few people have bothered to count them, and partly because the criteria are so various—total absence of speech may or may not co-exist with considerable comprehension, with use of gestures, non-verbal vocalizations, facial expressions, and other forms of reciprocal social communication. Also the overlap with 'autism' is very great. Since the diagnosis of the latter condition is very various and selective, differential categorization at this level of handicap is often more a matter of institutional and personal traditions than of differences between the patients. However the numbers of non-speaking subnormals is certainly much greater in hospitals than in 'community' homes, training centres, or hostels. King, Raynes and Tizard (1971) estimate more than half of all inmates have no effective speech or understanding. To what extent these figures reflect the undoubted fact that hospitals take a much higher proportion of the most handicapped, and to what extent they reflect the adverse effect most hospital environments have on language skills, is unknown; clearly both factors are involved.

Largely by definition non-speaking subnormals tend to be those with the lowest IQ scores, though there are exceptions in both directions to this. Knowledge of the possible 'causes' of failure to acquire language is largely speculative, both at a general level and in any particular case. There has been little extensive neurological investigation of the low grade subnormal, and as far as can be ascertained, cases where neurological damage could be a sufficient explanation of failure to speak are proportionately not all that common. However ignorance is almost total in this area. Neurological factors associated with extremely slow development, e.g. loss of plasticity of the nervous system with relatively great chronological age, may also be relevant. However Buddenhagen's (1917) success in teaching an eighteen-year-old inmate to speak provides evidence against this in one particular case. Low intelligence itself is sometimes cited as a cause of inability to acquire any useful language but it is never made clear quite what the causal connection is supposed to be or indeed the cause.

On a Piagetian model of language development it could be hypothesized that some individuals don't acquire language because they have not developed sufficiently in other non-verbal respects, e.g. object permanence, delayed imitation. The problem with such a developmental approach is that on a general level it is quite likely to be true. There are individuals whose development is so grossly retarded that they have not progressed beyond a few basic sensory-motor functions and therefore would not be expected to show any representative skills. However at a more specific level there is no empirical evidence at all concerning the kinds of developmental connections Piaget was postulating between verbal and prior non-verbal development (Ryan, 1974a), or even for any inevitable succession in time of the supposed events. Descriptions of the abilities of subnormal individuals in Piagetian terms do not seem to shed much light on the problem of whether there is some developmental stage that the majority of non-speakers can be said not to have attained, and which can be considered necessary for language development. This lack of satisfactory descriptive work is probably partly to do with the well-known problems with the definition of Piagetian 'stages', but partly also because of the difficulty of applying tasks and skills evolved for infants to fully grown, often ambulant, grossly retarded individuals. This once again highlights the difficulties of applying notions of 'normal' development to subnormal people, whose skills may develop in a completely different way, if at all.

On a Chomskian model of language acquisition, apart from Chomsky's (1968) somewhat obscure statement that language acquisition is independent of intelligence level (apparently made to emphasize the species-specificity of language), the failure to acquire language could be seen as some deficiency in the innate equipment, or in its application. The problem with the general Chomsky position is that it is not obvious why *any* specific deficiency in the LAD should be associated with low intelligence, and therefore difficult to predict what kinds of deficiencies to expect with subnormals. However one extrapolation might be that syntax rather than lexical knowledge would be the most sensitive area, which has to some extent been corroborated by the findings cited above in the last section. This however is not relevant to total failure to talk.

A generalized Skinnerian position tends of course to emphasize the environmental deficiencies surrounding a subnormal individual. Its greatest application has been in various remediation and training programs (see below). Its undoubted relevance in these areas does not really contribute to any explanatory account of the pre-existing failure, though it can of course show how absence of language is positively reinforced, especially in institutional settings. Its lack of explanatory relevance is due to the absence of any adequate conceptualization of what a child is acquiring in the way of skills, and the developmental processes involved.

All that can really be said at present about the failure of language development in many subnormals is that the causes must be many and various, both between and within individuals. This complexity is well brought out by Buddenhagen's monograph (1971). Here pre-existing physiological defects (in these cases possibly impaired hearing, frequently blocked respiration and consequent difficulty in phonation) are compounded with very unhelpful environments, and in some cases, with excessive medication. A child of 'normal' intelligence might be more able to learn despite these disadvantages; anyhow he would be much less likely to be subjected to them. Subnormal children are much more likely in the first place to have various physiological and neurological defects than 'normal' children. In the second place they are more vulnerable to their adverse effects. In the third place, for the reason described above in the last section, they are more likely to produce an unhelpful human environment for themselves by the way they behave; and even if they don't do so, the chances that others will are much greater than with less vulnerable 'normal' children. In these circumstances, which could be indefinitely multiplied, it is a waste of time and money to look for single sufficient causes, or to categorize non-speakers into discrete types according to presumed causation.

Operant conditioning programs of many kinds are now widespread and extremely fashionable especially in residential institutions. Behaviour modification is fast becoming part of the philosophy of management of institutions, as opposed to an educational extra. Nurses are trained in it not just for special training units but as part of their whole ward behaviour. Operant conditioning techniques have frequently been employed as a response to the crisis of overcrowding, understaffing, degrading conditions, and violent behaviour of both patients and staff (see Thompson and Grabowski, 1972). It has both its liberating and repressive aspects, and can only be evaluated within the context that it is applied, since this context dictates what behaviour is trained or extinguished and with what consequences. Behaviour modification can undoubtedly liberate a severely subnormal individual from a state of incontinence, from his or her inability to feed or dress him or herself, from self-destructive behaviour such as scratching or head-banging. It can also liberate the nurses from having to tend to these matters, and other patients from violent attacks. Few people would deny that such minimal independence, with all the experiences that this then makes possible, is a desirable end. Unfortunately we cannot ask the person whose behaviour is conditioned what he or she feels about it—it may be that being dressed and toileted by a nurse are the only pleasurable and sensuous experiences of a barren life, and that the 'freedom' to go to the much less sensuous occupational therapy, for example, as a result of becoming continent and more independent, is no compensation—who knows? Nor do any operant programs give the patient an effective choice about whether to participate, or about what is taught to him or her. The range of behaviour selected is usually determined by the demands of the ward and hospital situation, and by implicit standards of what is socially desirable and acceptable.

Language programs as yet are only a small part of the extensive literature on behaviour modification—this may be because it is more difficult to carry out successfully, or because it is more difficult to train nurses to do so, or because it is a low priority in hospital settings. For various reasons it is not possible to present a comprehensive account of the successes and failures of various approaches. This is partly because the operant literature is characterized by an excessive ratio of theoretical and methodological preliminaries to details of results and conclusions—surely it is not necessary every time to reiterate the extremely well-known principles involved? Secondly the particular sequence of methods, reinforcements, responses, varies greatly from case to case, and has to be flexibly determined as the program proceeds rather than laid down beforehand. Thirdly the non-speaking subjects involved vary enormously in their residual capacities, histories, ages etc. and in many unknown ways. Lastly failure may consist either in no change within the experimental setting, or else in change that is not carried over into other contexts, or that disappears with withdrawal reinforcement. Unlike most other ward programs which are carried out in the setting where the behaviour is normally required, language programs seem usually to require training in a separate context, outside other activities. In general we do not know enough about the cases and circumstances where change in verbal skills is *not* achieved; and we do not have adequate follow-up descriptions of the social use of speech that has been taught.

The methods used have been developed from those first employed with autistic children. Most programs emphasize the necessity of first obtaining sustained visual attention to the experimenter's face, but tend to differ on the necessity for establishing non-vocal motor imitation before training vocal and verbal imitation. Some have argued for the establishment of a general imitative repertoire before attempting specific imitation of mouth movements and sounds (e.g. Baer *et al.*, 1972; Risley *et al.*, 1972). All programs appear to use some kind of model-echo paradigm, starting with component speech sounds that are then chained into words, and these into phrases. Some programs follow ideas of phonological complexity or natural development in choosing which speech sounds and words to train first of all, others simply choose what sounds and words seem most immediately useful. Imitation is then phased out in favour either of object labelling or of verbal prompts and answers to questions. Here again the succession of speech functions is not based on any particular theory of what happens 'naturally'. It should be noted that nothing that happens or fails to happen, in speech programs of any kind, has any necessary implications about what happens 'normally', or about what has failed to happen.

In general, behaviour modification has worked like nothing else has ever worked in this area, whatever the particular failures. One should however keep alive the question of whether the sometimes extremely coercive methods justify the ends (see some of the case histories in Browning and Storer, 1971, for example). Unfortunately such issues are always seen as separate from the 'technical' questions of how to bring about behavioural change more efficiently. Our power over the lives of these people is total, and the fact that we have now found a technology for exercising this power more efficiently than formerly, and often to their presumed benefit, does not in any way alter the power relations involved. We also need, as noted above, more information on subsequent social use of language and the development of more complex language skills 'attempts to produce 'appropriate' social speech are not very common. Barton's (1973) attempt to get already verbal inmates to talk to each other failed when reinforcement was withdrawn. This is hardly surprising since it is unlikely they had very much to talk about apart from the reinforcement dispenser and the experimenter, which is what they mostly talked about when reinforced. The three patients in question had spent years living together in hospital and spent a large part of each uneventful day sitting round the same table, also together. How much would any of us 'normals' have to say to each other in such conditions? Wouldn't we also exhibit language 'deficits'?

Baer, D. M., Guess, D. and Sherman, J. A. (1972). In Schiefelbusch, R. L. (Ed.), *Language of the mentally retarded*. Baltimore: University Park Press.

Barton, E. S. (1973). Operant conditioning of appropriate and inappropriate social speech in the profoundly retarded. *Journal of Mental Deficiency Research*, **17**, 183-91.

Baumeister, A. A. (1968). Behavioral inadequacy and variability of performance. *American Journal of Mental Deficiency*, **73**, 477-83.

Beier, E. G., Startweather, J. A. and Lambert, M. J. (1969). Vocabulary usage of mentally retarded children. *American Journal of Mental Deficiency*, **73**, 927-34.

Belmont, J. (1971). In Ellis, N. R. (Ed.), *International review of research in mental retardation*, vol. 5, New York: Academic Press.

Birch, H. G., Belmont, L., Belmont, I. and Taft, L. (1967). Brain damage and intelligence in educable mentally subnormal children. *Journal of Nervous and Mental Disorders*, 247-57.

Brown, R., Cazden, C. R. and Bellugi, U. (1969). Child's grammar from I to III. In Hill, J. P. (Ed.), *Minnesota symposium on child psychology*. Minneapolis, Minn.: University of Minnesota Press.

Browning, R. M. and Storer, D. O. (1971). *Behavior modification in child treatment*. Chicago: Aldine.

Bryant, P. (1970). In Richards, B. W. (Ed.), *Mental subnormality*. London: Pitman.

Buddenhagen, R. G. (1971). *Establishing vocal verbalizations in mute mongoloid children*. Champaign, Illinois: Research Press Co.

Carr, J. (1970). Mental and motor development in young mongol children. *Journal of Mental Deficiency Research*, **14**, 205-20.

Chomsky, N. (1968). *Language and mind*. New York: Harcourt, Brace and World, Inc.

Clarke, A. M. and Clarke, A. D. B. (1967). In Zubin, J. (Ed.), *Psycho-pathology of mental development*. New York: Grace and Stratton.

Cooper, E. (1976). A discussion of how teachers behave towards the stupid child. In Wadsworth, M. (Ed.), *Studies in everyday medical life*. In Press.

Cunningham, C. (1974). In Tizard, J. (Ed.), *Mental retardation: concepts of education and research*. London: Butterworth.

Dever, R. B. and Gardner, W. I. (1970). Performance of normal and retarded boys in Berko's test of morphology, *Language and Speech*. **13**, 162-81.

Edgerton, R. B. (1967). *The cloak of competence*. Berkeley: University of California Press.

Evans, D. and Hampson, M. (1968). The language of mongols. *British Journal of Disorders of Communication*. 171-81.

Fenn, G. (1973). The development of syntax in a group of severely sub-normal children. Ph.D. thesis, Cambridge University.

Fulton, R. T. and Lloyd, L. L. (1968). Hearing impairment in a population of children with Down's syndrome. *American Journal of Mental Deficiency*. **73**, 298-302.

Garfield, J. C., Benton, A. L. and MacQueen, J. C. (1966). Motor impersistence in brain-damaged and cultural-familial defectives. *Journal of Nervous and Mental Disorders*. **142**, 434-40.

Graham, J. T. and Graham, L. W. (1971). Language behaviour of the mentally retarded: syntactic characteristics. *American Journal of Mental Deficiency*, **75**, 623-9.

Inhelder, B. (1943). *The diagnosis of reasoning in the mentally retarded*. Trans. 1968. New York: John Day Co.

Jeffree, D. M. (1974). In Tizard, J. (Ed.), *Mental retardation: concepts of education and research*. London: Butterworth.

Jeffree, D. M. and Cashdan, A. (1971). Severely subnormal children and their parents—an experiment in language improvement. *British Journal of Educational Psychology*. **41**, 184.

Jordan, R. E. (1967). Language and mental retardation. In Schiefelbusch, R. L., Copeland, R. H. and Smith, J. O. (Eds.), *Language and mental retardation*. New York: Holt.

King, R. D., Raynes, N. and Tizard, J. (1971). *Patterns of residential care*. London: Routledge.

Kounin, J. S. (1941). Experimental studies of rigidity. *Character and Personality*, **9**, 251-72.

Lackner, J. R. (1968). A developmental study of language behaviour in retarded children. *Neuropsychologia*, **6**, 301-20.

Lenneberg, E. H., Nichols, I. A. and Rosenberger, E. F. (1964). Primitive stages of language development in mongolism. In *Disorders of communication*, vol. XLII. A.R.N.M.D.

Lloyd, L. L. and Fulton, R. T. (1972). In McLean, J. E. *et al.* (Eds.), *Language intervention with the retarded*. Baltimore: University Park Press.

Lyle, J. G. (1960). The effect of an institution environment upon the verbal development of imbecile children. *Journal of Mental Deficiency Research*, **4**, 1-13.

Lyle, J. G. (1961). A comparison of the language of normal and imbecile children. *Journal of Mental Deficiency Research*, **5**, 40-51.

McLean, J. E., Yoder, D. E. and Schiefelbusch, R. L. (Eds.) (1972). *Language intervention with the retarded*. Baltimore: University Park Press.

Mannoni, M. (1964). *The backward child and his mother*. Trans. 1972. New York: Pantheon.

Marshall, N. R., Hegreves, J. R. and Goldstein, S. (1973). Mothers and their retarded children vs. mothers and their non-retarded children. *American Journal of Mental Deficiency*, **77**, 415-19.

Mein, R. (1961). A study of the oral vocabularies of severely subnormal patients. *Journal of Mental Deficiency Research*, **5**, 52-62.

Morris, G. (1975). In O'Connor, N. (Ed.), *Language cognitive deficit and retardation*. IRMR Study Group No. 7, London: Butterworth.

O'Connor, N. and Hermelin, B. (1963). *Speech and thought in severe subnormality*. London: Pergamon.

Risley, T., Hart, B. and Doke, L. (1972). In Schiefelbusch, R. L. (Ed.), *Language of the mentally retarded*. Baltimore: University Park Press.

Ryan, J. F. (1973a). In Clarke, A. D. B. and Clarke, A. M. (Eds.), *Mental retardation and behavioural research*. London: Churchill Livingstone.

Ryan, J. F. (1973b). In Mittler, P. (Ed.), *Assessment for learning in the mentally handicapped*. London: Churchill Livingstone.

Ryan, J. F. (1973c). In Hinde, R. A. and Hinde, J. S. (Eds.), *Constraints on learning—limitations and predispositions*. London: Academic Press.

Ryan, J. F. (1974). In Richards, M. P. M. (Ed.), *The integration of the child in the social world*. Cambridge: Cambridge University Press.

Ryan, J. F. (1976). Some remarks on the involvement of medicine and psychology in the production and management of stupidity. In Wadsworth, M. (Ed.), *Studies in everyday medical life*. In Press.

Segal, S. S. (1966). *Backward children in the USSR*. London: Arnold.

Semmel, M. I., Barritt, L. S., Bennett, S. W. and Perfetti, C. A. (1968). A grammatical analysis of word associations of educable mentally retarded and normal children. *American Journal of Mental Deficiency*, **72**, 567-76.

Spradlin, J. E. (1963). Language and communication of mental defectives. In Ellis, N. R. (Ed.), *Handbook of mental deficiency*. New York: McGraw Hill.

Spradlin, J. E. and Rosenberg, S. (1964). Complexity of adult verbal behaviour in a dyadic situation with retarded children. *Journal of Abnormal and Social Psychology*, **58**, 694-8.

Thompson, T. and Grabowski, J. (Eds.) (1972). *Behavior modification of the mentally retarded*. New York: Oxford University Press.

Disorders in the Expression of Language

JOHN C. MARSHALL
*Research Director, Interfakultaire Werkgroep Taal-en
Spraakgedrag, University of Nijmegen*

126

CONTENTS

The primary goal of neurolinguistic inquiry can be simply stated: the discipline seeks to understand the form of representation of language in the human brain. An adequate theory might be expected to pair an information-processing account of psycholinguistic functions with a detailed statement of the physiological realization of those functions in terms of neuronal circuitry (and whatever non-neuronal principles of electro-chemical pattern formation that may be found appropriate to the description of central nervous system states).

Yet although a considerable body of observations has been accumulated concerning the types of language deficit which may result from injury to the mature brain, it is widely held that these observations have, so far, eluded systematic explanation. Rosenblith's lament—'Why are we so data-rich and so theory-poor?'—seems to be an appropriate comment on the state of the art in neurolinguistics (Rosenblith, 1967). More sweeping criticisms, although again made more in sorrow than in anger, are not difficult to find. In their *magnum opus* which reviews the last fifteen years' work in the psychology of language, Fodor, Bever and Garrett (1974) remark:

It is the sad truth that remarkably little has been learned about the psychology of language processes in normals from over a hundred years of aphasia study, and that nothing at all has been learned about possible neurological realizations of language from the psycholinguistic advances which this book will survey. (p. XIV)

Taxonomic neurolinguistics as represented by the discovery of correlations between varieties of dysphasia and injury to (relatively) restricted cortical areas is not, one might claim, an enterprise which bears comparison with, say, our knowledge of the functions of the cerebellum in the control of movement and postural adjustment (Eccles, 1973).

Although I find myself in broad agreement with such views (Caplan and Marshall, 1975), I shall argue in the following section that the situation is not quite as gloomy as the above account implies (at least with respect to the first of Fodor *et al.*'s claims). In an endeavour to substantiate my optimism, I shall take a restricted area of investigation—the description of disorders of spontaneous language production in adults—and I shall try to show how aphasiological evidence can suggest plausible hypotheses concerning this process. I shall also hint at how such data might be used in choosing between alternative theories of linguistic expression. Firstly, however, a general approach to the problem must be outlined.

Fodor *et al.* summarize their views on the framework within which studies of sentence production may profitably be conducted in the following paragraph:

We have assumed that speech production is a matter of computing a sequence of encodings of a message; that this sequence starts with a representation which formally characterizes the speaker's communicative intent; and that it ends with a surface form. The first is presumed to be at least as abstract a representation as linguistic semantics provides for sentences and to be in the language in which central data processing occurs. The last is assumed to be interpretable as a sequence of instructions to the vocal apparatus. (p. 434)

Although the beginning and end of the process are fixed in this way, the intervening steps are, of course, the unknowns in the operation. And it is, as Fodor *et al*, remark, an empirical problem to discover what 'interlevels of encoding' occur, and in what order they are computed. One notion of *levels* is specified in linguistic theory, where distinctions might be drawn between, for example, syntactic, phonemic and phonetic levels of organization. But there is no reason to assume that the order of levels found in the *generation* of sentences by explicit theories of linguistic structure (Chomsky, 1965; Fillmore, 1968) parallels the sequence of operations in the *production* of utterances. Indeed, there is no *a priori* reason why *linguistic* levels should play any crucial role in this latter procedure. There is, however, some experimental evidence (from normal subjects) in support of the hypothesis that surface structure trees (in the sense of Chomsky, 1957, 1965) are implicated in the production of utterances, and that, furthermore, these trees are constructed from left to right, top to bottom, and clause by clause. This is (almost) the only substantive proposal concerning sentence production to which Fodor, Bever and Garrett are prepared to commit themselves.

Data consistent with the conjecture—which is essentially a modified version of Yngve's depth hypothesis (1960)—are discussed at some length by Fodor *et al*. (1974), pp. 406-34. Such trees—construed as syntactic objects elaborated under the control of semantic representations—will then, at very least, be further transcribed into a phonological code which is in turn interpretable as an articulatory program (Fromkin, 1968).

The issue now arises: can the paradigm that Fodor *et al.* propose encompass what is known about disorders of language and speech production consequent upon cortical and subcortical brain injury? And if so, can these disorders of expressive language provide information which will begin to fill out the rough outline given above? While trying to sketch answers to these questions, my primary concern will be to illustrate something of the variety of expressive disorders to which any model of language production must ultimately be responsive.

Let us now begin at the beginning—where the most difficult problems lie—with the notion of communicative intent.

A STARTING MECHANISM?

For the normal adult, communicative intent is frequently expressed through a spoken language, although it is obvious that such intent may be expressed in other ways, ways which include such semi-conventional facial and bodily gestures as eyebrow raising, shrugs and pointing. In some situations, fairly complex information may be carried non-verbally. I can, for instance, reply quite precisely to your question 'How do I get to Waverley Station?' by drawing you a map—either in the air or on paper. Whilst performances of this nature have considerable structure—they can be described by rules—there is presumably a rather limited similarity between the grammar of such an act and the grammar of an appropriate linguistic response. (Both, however, may presuppose an ontology which includes, for example, agents, acts, objects and goals.) One might argue, then, that the first step in *language* production is indeed the decision that the linguistic system be activated in preference (or in addition) to non-verbal modes of expression.

The phenomenon of akinetic mutism (Cairns, Oldfield, Penny-backer and Whitteridge, 1941) has sometimes been interpreted as a specific impairment of such a 'switch-on' device. Thus although akinetic mutism may occur as '. . . one aspect of a general failure to act' (Geschwind, 1964), patients have been observed with a more or less total mutism in the context of relatively well-preserved comprehension (as assessed by the ability to carry out simple commands), preserved general motility, and the ability to reply appropriately to questions by gesture (e.g. raising one finger for 'Yes' and two for 'No'). The absence of neurological signs indicating, for example, facial apraxia or pseudobulbar palsy supports the diagnosis; the absence of psychiatric signs would rule out hysterical mutism; and the course of recovery does not usually show the types of articulatory, phonologic and syntactic disorders which are characteristic of the remission of severe motor aphasia.

These relatively 'pure' forms of akinetic mutism accordingly lead Botez (1962) to speculate on the existence of a 'starting mechanism of speech', impairment of which may be seen after lesions (focal or diffuse) at many different levels of the central nervous system. (One might wish to generalize 'speech' to 'language' for the initiation of verbal expression in the written mode would appear to be equally affected. And where gesture is no longer used to impart information the condition would have to be described as a total failure of communicative intent.) These patients, quite unlike the severe motor aphasic, may give little or no evidence (by way of grimaces, lip and tongue movements) of even *trying* to speak. One of Botez' patients, following recovery some ten days after the removal of a left-hemisphere (frontal) tumor, was asked why he had not spoken; he replied: 'I felt too lazy to speak.'

Some 'mute' patients do, however, produce some speech, for example answering 'Yes' or 'No' upon repeated questioning; similarly a patient may manage to write down his name and address. And here we do see a similarity between akinetic mutism and such conditions as global aphasia and 'motor' aphasia. Even the most severely affected 'speechless' patient will, typically, be able to produce some utterances within a few days or at most weeks post injury. Broca's second patient, Lelong (Broca, 1861), could reply 'Oui' and 'Non' in an appropriate fashion. To all questions which demanded a numerical answer he gave 'Tois' (trois); he gave 'Lelo' when asked his name, and 'Toujours' in reply to all other questions. It has frequently been noted that stock phrases, greetings, and taboo expressions are often retained by the patient who is otherwise totally incapacitated in spontaneous speech. Bastian (1897) reports a patient whose language-production was limited to 'Yes', 'No', 'Yes, I know' and 'Goodnight'. Charles Baudelaire ended his days at the Institute of Saint-Jean able to utter no more than 'Cré nom' (Sacré nom de Dieu). Stock phrases may be used in all contexts, appropriate and inappropriate alike. Bateman (1892) describes a patient who invariably replied 'The other day' to any question whatsoever: 'I asked her how many children she had; she replied, "The other day." She could say nothing else, and this recurring utterance, whether appropriate or not, she repeated on all occasions.'

The preservation of so-called *serial-speech* has likewise been noted. That is, patients whose spontaneous communicative skills are almost non-existent (and who sometimes cannot even repeat a word or a phrase said to them by the examiner) may adequately recite such 'overlearned', redundant sequences as a list of months of the year, the numbers from one to ten, or indeed a whole nursery rhyme or prayer from the Bible (Rommel, 1683). In so doing, the patient may display quite acceptable articulatory and prosodic control of his speech. The patient who can recite from one to twenty but not from twenty to one (Kleist, 1934; Isserlin, 1922) is clearly not suffering from a phonologic or articulatory difficulty *tout court*.

With such dissociations in mind, Hughlings Jackson (1878) distinguished between *propositional* and *automatic* speech, regarding the above patterns of loss and retention as a failure in the ability to propositionalize; for Jackson this notion has the connotation of constructing novel but appropriate utterances in which sound and sense are linked by choices made on the levels of semantics and syntax. He writes (1874): 'Speaking is not simply the *utterance* of words . . . it consists of words *referring to one another in a particular manner*; and without a proper inter-relation of its parts a verbal utterance would be a mere succession of names embodying no proposition.' Jackson encapsulates his distinction in the aphorism: 'The Communist orator did not really make a blunder when he began his oration, "Thank God, I am an Atheist".'

Aphasic subjects who retain the impulse to speak may nonetheless only be capable of producing utterances which come 'pre-packed' rather than unfolded under the guidance of syntactic and semantic plans. Linguistic units are defined basically by their contrastive function, but control over choices at different levels in the linguistic hierarchy is precisely what is lost in the most severely affected aphasic subjects. Aphasic stereotypes may *appear* to be quite complex (as, for example, in Alajouanine's patient, 1956, whose recurring utterance was 'Bonsoir, les choses d'ici-bas') but their unvarying form reflects their lack of internal organization; they are, in Hughlings Jackson's phrase 'ready made speech'.

Although the broad terms of the distinction between propositional and automatic language are fairly clear, there is no adequate formal account of the cline between them, no account of how the '. . . automatic use of words *merges into voluntary use of words*' (Hughlings Jackson, 1874). The point that Jackson makes here applies, of course, to all other units of linguistic analysis. This general issue may have practical relevance to attempts to quantify rate of recovery from aphasia. One might expect that the notions of distributional and sequential redundancy, in their traditional information-theoretic sense, would be useful tools in the attempt to characterize the continuum. A number of difficulties arise, however, when such measures are extended beyond simple linear orderings in order to cover hierarchical systems of the type required in the description of language (but see Banerji, 1963). The whole area of heterogenous speech modes is summarized most expertly by Van Lancker (1975).

ELEMENTARY PROPOSITIONS

During the further course of recovery, automatic speech may be supplemented (or replaced) by utterances which—however deviant they may be—are clearly attempts to convey information appropriate to the situation. In patients with frontal lesions a condition known as 'expressive agrammatism' is frequently seen. Lexical words—nouns, adjectives and main verbs—are to be found in the patient's speech, although his active vocabulary may be small (Cohen and Hecaen, 1965); but there is a drastic reduction in the frequency of grammatical formatives relative to their occurrence in normal speech. This decrease applies both to free-standing forms, such as articles, and to bound elements from the inflectional system (Geschwind and Howes, 1962). In extreme cases it would seem that all expression is reduced to nominal form. For example, a patient seen by Dercum (1894) is asked to detail the history of his early life; he produces the following utterance: 'School, marbles, farm, errands, engineer, Glasgow, Philadelphia'.

The subject has provided a reasonably clear and informative account, despite the apparently total inability to produce overtly even the simplest grammatical structures. Dercum reports that, very occasionally, the patient did manage a short sentence containing the verbs 'was' or 'make'.

In addition to the loss—more or less severe—of grammatical structure in spontaneous speech, the frontal aphasias are frequently characterized by a variety of 'output' disorders. There is a reduction in the amount of speech produced per unit time; articulation is laborious and frank phonetic and phonemic errors may be made; intonational patterns are disturbed (Goodglass, Quadfasel and Timberlake, 1964; Monrad-Krohn, 1947); hence the term 'non-fluent' aphasia. Given the above syndrome it is not surprising that, although agrammatism can obviously be *described* in syntactic terms, most scholars have emphasized a combination of phonologic and semantic variables in their explanations of the condition. Some of the relevant phonologic distortions are noted above; semantic factors are then introduced when patients are described as retaining the use of 'content' words to a greater extent than the use of 'function' words. Use of the metaphor 'telegraphic style' will usually indicate such an approach (Luria, 1958). The term may be spelt out in the following fashion.

The point of telegram-writing—by normal subjects—is to maximize the 'informativeness' of a communication whilst keeping 'cost' to a minimum. Subjects with agrammatism give the appearance of knowing what they want to say and of trying to say it; in classical cases (e.g. Salomon, 1914), comprehension of language is relatively well-preserved, and this may be taken as evidence that knowledge of linguistic form is intact (although the data of Zurif, Caramazza and Myerson, 1972, suggests that *some* non-fluent aphasics do suffer receptive loss for the forms they find difficult to express). However, the laborious, distorted and frequently paraphasic quality of the motor aphasic's speech suggests that the cost of expressing this knowledge has risen; communication is effortful. What, then, more reasonable than that verbal elements having a high cost to information ratio should fail to be overtly expressed (although not, of course, by conscious design on the subject's part)?

It is in this spirit that Wepman and Jones (1964) write: '. . . the disorder, even in its most extreme manifestations, seldom seriously interferes with the ability to communicate meaningfully and effectively'. Such a position may easily become exaggerated, however, as one can see from the examples that Wepman and Jones themselves quote:

Examiner: 'Where is your daughter?'
Patient: 'New Orleans . . . home . . . Monday.'
Examiner: 'Will she stay home?'
Patient: 'No . . . no . . . bridesmaid . . . working . . . married . . . no.'

The patient's first response may be construed as 'New Orleans is her home', but the significance of 'Monday' is opaque; alternatively, the utterance may be a version of 'New Orleans (is where she is now). She will be home on Monday.' In either case, it is impossible to tell from the patient's second response whether the daughter is about to be married or is to be a bridesmaid at someone else's wedding. Nonetheless, the telegram metaphor does seem apt, and patients will indeed frequently convey the 'gist' of a message with some facility. The following example illustrates this; a patient, reported by Tissot, Mounin, and Lhermitte (1973), is describing a series of pictures which concern a boy's adventures with a red balloon:

Vois, voir . . . achète ballon . . . rouge . . . m'amuser . . . content monter en haut . . . après ici . . . content . . . ballon alors couché . . . hélas ici . . . ballon . . . cassé . . . ou . . . chais pas quoi . . . alors . . . ici . . . rien . . . mystère . . . et pleure parce que ballon . . . cassé pi . . . pleure.

Although appropriate nouns, adjectives, main verbs, adverbials, and *some* function words (après, ou, et, parce que) are to be found in this passage, pronouns, auxiliary verbs and articles are conspicuous by their absence.

As it stands, however, the telegram metaphor is descriptive rather than explanatory; it can be interpreted in (at least) two distinct ways when incorporated into a sequential analysis of 'the path from thought to speech' (Pick, 1931). Telegramese can be seen either as a failure in the construction of a (surface) syntactic representation, or as a failure in the transcription of elements during the translation from surface structure to phonological realization.

Assume a situation in which the sentence 'A man is returning the books' could appropriately be uttered; assume that what is actually said is 'Man return book'. In line with the first hypothesis (Pick, 1913), we might propose an account of the following kind: a semantic representation determines a 2-place function, f (x,y) for 'conveying' the content *return* (man, books); this formula is elaborated into the 'deepish' structure (cf. Jacobs and Rosenbaum, 1968):

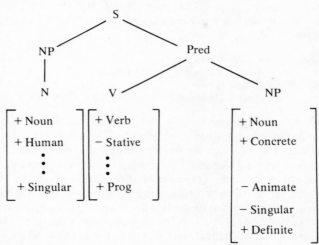

No further elaboration of structure takes place; what becomes overtly realized is the closest monomorphemic approximation to the semantic representations associated with the final entries in the above tree. In some cases, lexical items may be inserted at too high a node. Thus when patients omit main verbs from their utterances one could argue that noun phrase objects have been inserted at the predicate node without 'waiting' for the V⌒NP expansion to take place. Goodglass, Gleason, Bernholtz and Hyde (1972) report examples, 'I . . . uh . . . motorcycles', which are consistent with the above suggestion. (The proposal does, of course, require that nouns be specified in the lexicon as *predicates*. The form of deep-structure representation outlined by Bach, 1968, would provide structures appropriate to the operation of such an 'early insertion' strategy.)

On the second hypothesis, however, a quite different picture emerges. A full *surface* tree is constructed:

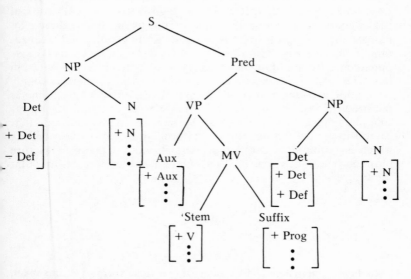

But in the translation from semantics and syntax to phonology and phonetic representation certain items (including, for example, those which do not receive main stress) are 'deleted' (or, better, fail to be transcribed).

The contrast, then, is this: hypothesis 1; lexical insertion takes place (and the final articulatory program is activated) *before* a (full) surface form is constructed: hypothesis 2; transcription from (surface) syntactic structure to phonological (and/or articulatory) form is liable to error. These two positions have parallels in the literature on language acquisition (Braine, 1974) where they can be seen in the interpretation of 'holophrastic' utterances. (This suggests that the issue is relevant to Jakobson's claim, 1941, that the patterns of dissolution in aphasia mirror the child's original acquisition of language.) What evidence could enable a choice to be made between these hypotheses (or, of course, force one into some kind of compromise position)?

Goodglass and Berko (1960) have observed cases of non-fluent aphasia in which syllabic variants of grammatical inflections are easier to produce than their non-syllabic counterparts; they did not find such a pattern in cases of fluent aphasia. The non-fluent aphasic is thus more likely to omit the plural, third person singular, and past tense markers from words such as *books, runs,* and *played* than from *horses, catches, waited* etc. There are a variety of ways in which such a result could be obtained, but they must *all* be variations on hypothesis 2. It is a fact of English that the realization of the category *Noun Plural* (in regular nouns by one of the three allomorphs /-z/, /-s/, or /-iz/) is phonologically conditioned; realization of the category *Past Tense* (by /-t/, /-d/, or /-id/) is likewise phonologically conditioned. On the level of syntactic representation (e.g. *Base Noun⌢Plural,* or *Verb Stem⌢Past Tense*) there is simply no way of marking which allomorph of the inflectional ending is required. (Consider, for example, the verbs 'to end' and 'to finish'. The phonological composition of the final segments, and only that composition, determines the overt form of the *past tense* ending which is required in each case. Syntactic and semantic structure plays no role in this specification.) One must therefore assume that the subtrees

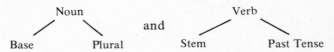

have been constructed. But once the lexical formative has been specified phonologically, one can state, for example, that when the stem ends in an alveolar stop then there is a high probability that the inflection will be realized (that is, found in the overt response), and conversely it can be stated that there is a low probability of realization when the stem ends in a sibilant. A similar type of argument applies to the allomorphs of the third person singular inflection on verbs; thus Goodglass, Gleason, Bernholtz and Hyde (1972) describe a patient who fairly consistently fails to mark the /-s/ variant (e.g. 'laughs' → 'laugh') but who shows far greater success on /-iz/, as in *chases*. (Greater economy will, of course, be achieved if such regularities are stated over a distinctive feature rather than a phonemic representation. This does not, however, affect the argument under consideration.) For some aphasic subjects, then, the factor of 'phonological prominence' (Goodglass, 1968) may make syllabic variants and forms which can (in certain contexts) take main stress easier to realize.

Yet it would appear that this line of reasoning will not work for all cases of 'motor' aphasia, and perhaps not even for all examples of agrammatism within a single individual (de Villiers, 1974). For example, Myerson and Goodglass (1972) report on a patient who *always* succeeds in marking regular nouns for number (i.e. invariably produces the correct inflection when any of the three forms /-s/, /-z/ and /-iz/ is required); the patient, however, *never* marks third person singular (whatever the requisite allomorph). But the phonological conditioning and the realizations of the allomorphs are *identical* for the noun and the verb inflections. There is thus no way in which the contrast between (total) success on nouns and (total) failure on verbs can be stated at the level of phonological representation. We must accordingly assume that the category *noun* is expanded to *base⌢number* but that *verbal* is not rewritten as *stem⌢affix*. Myerson and Goodglass point out that, in this patient's speech, 'subject and verb never appear in the same utterance'; his remarks are always of the form *noun phrase* or *verb phrase*, never *noun phrase⌢verb phrase*. They consider this fact related to the absence of /-s/, /-z/, and /-iz/ on verbs; '. . . and hence there is no instance of verbal inflection to agree with a subject in the third person singular when the verb is in the present tense'. Their use of 'hence' is justified if and only if one makes the following kinds of assumption: when the patient produces an utterance under the structural description *verb phrase*, a *noun phrase* subject constituent was never constructed; or a *noun phrase*, although never overtly expressed was elaborated to the level of its base form but no further; or a *noun phrase* was elaborated to the level of < + Third Person : + Singular > but this specification was never 'copied' to a position behind the verb stem. These possibilities are all variants of hypothesis 1. And indeed it would seem that this hypothesis must be invoked (in addition to hypothesis 2) for the patient described by Goodglass *et al.* (1972). For although this patient does find syllabic forms easier than non-syllabic ones, there is also a grammatical hierarchy of difficulty; plurals are marked correctly more frequently than either possessives or third person singular.

Data from agrammatic subjects permit, albeit tentatively, the following generalizations (Jakobson, 1964); noun inflections (plural and possessive) are more likely to be expressed than verb inflections (past tense and third person agreement). There is also an effect due to level in the syntactic hierarchy; thus *plural* and *past tense* markings (i.e. agreement at the word level) are easier than *possessive* and *third person* markings (i.e. agreement at the phrase and sentence levels, respectively).

Attempts to explain the quality of agrammatic speech solely in terms of phonologic and articulatory variables will run foul of other observations. For example, subjects do not typically leave out from 'content' words unstressed medial syllables which have no morphological significance; yet in Japanese, a language in which some case markers are infixed, these grammatical infixes are frequently omitted by 'motor' aphasics (Panse and Shimoyama, 1955). To take another example from a non Indo-European language, Ndebele, a Bantu language very closely related to Zulu, has an elaborate system of alliterative concord which can be stated in the following (much simplified) manner: each noun stem has a fixed prefix whose overt expression is obligatory in well-formed sentences; the prefix of a head noun must appear on all forms (e.g. adjectives, verbs, possessive markers) which are governed by (i.e. are in construction with) that head noun. Traill (1970) has demonstrated that in a Ndebele speaker with motor aphasia and agrammatism these prefixes are quite frequently (although not invariably) incorrect or simply left out. Traill shows furthermore that the patient's speech contains no examples of 'an incorrect or zero noun prefix matched with a correct governed prefix'. Nouns with correct prefixes may, however, be accompanied by prefix errors, and by absence of prefixes, on governed forms. In other words, there is a relationship of *psychological* dependency which must make reference to the syntactic form of the expressed and the 'missing' elements.

I have noted above (and this is consistent with Traill's observations) that noun inflections are easier to express than verb inflections. It is known, however, that the progressive form *ing* causes few problems for the agrammatic subject; indeed, it may be the easiest of all English inflections for him (Myerson and Goodglass, 1972; de Villiers, 1974). *Prima facie,* this is a counter-example to the proposed regularity. The exception, however, is more apparent than real. Progressive aspect is part of the (optional) expansion of an auxiliary node, e.g. Chomsky's rule (1957):

$$Aux \rightarrow C(M) \ (have + en) \ (be + ing).$$

For present purposes it suffices to note that the progressive option is discontinuous, $(be + ing)$, requiring the correct choice of a form of *be* before the main verb in well-formed surface structures. But this is precisely what is *not* found in agrammatism. Although Myerson and Goodglass' patient A (1972) does produce utterances of the type *Main Verb ing*, the auxiliary *be* never appears in this construction. Schnitzer's patient (1974) sometimes uses the construction correctly —'I'm thinking', but he frequently omits one half or the other of the constituent—'You working in the rain', 'I'm help my cousin now.' The purported ease of expressing *progressive* (de Villiers, 1974) in subjects whose dialects require *be + ing* (but see Labov, 1969) is (half) illusory.

Nonetheless, it is certainly true that most agrammatic subjects do produce utterances of the type *verb‾ing*. If we assume that this is an erroneous version of the progressive, then the explanation for the pattern of loss and retention will presumably involve the fact that the correct choice of the overt form of *be* is conditioned by other parts of the structural description of the sentence ('I *am* going', 'You *are* going', 'He *is* going', 'I *was* going', 'You *were* going' etc.). Conditioning here is by tense and person, whereas *ing* is just *ing*.

In some instances, however, it is far from clear that the form is a representation of *progressive* at all; Myerson and Goodglass (1972) point out that the construction may be a nominalization. In transitive contexts, e.g. 'I driving a truck' (from Schnitzer, 1974), a nominal interpretation is perhaps unreasonable, but an utterance such as 'Baby crying' (from Goodglass *et al.*, 1972) may be susceptible to the analysis.

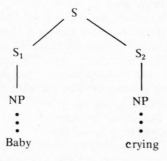

Bolinger (1961) makes this same point with respect to ordinary usage: '. . . when one motorist cuts ahead of another and the victim angrily mutters *That dirty dog—turning in front of me like that*, there is no way to tell which class the -ing belongs to.' The *general* plausibility of nominal interpretations may be increased by noting that verbs are frequently nominalized by aphasic subjects who are asked to read single words (Marshall, Newcombe and Marshall, 1970; Whitaker, 1972). Whitaker's corpus includes examples of gerundive nominals (*write* → writing) as well as agentive (*speak* → speaker) and derived nominals (*collect* → collection). Whitaker has also observed the phenomenon in sentence-construction tasks, e.g.

asked to use the word 'smile' in a sentence, patient W. L. produced (with a smile) 'I hate smiling'; given 'smoke', patient K. T. produced 'Smoking is not good for me'.

'Free-standing' function words (e.g. copula, auxiliary *do*, articles, modals, pronouns) also appear at a greatly reduced frequency in the speech of the agrammatic patient, indicating again that lack of syllabicity cannot be the sole variable determining which elements fail to appear in the patient's speech. The corpus from Myerson and Goodglass' (1972) patient A has no examples of the copula and no examples of articles (save for the indefinite in the context of constrained, measure phrases such as 'five hundred tons a day'). The subject does express cardinal numbers (including *one*) in prenominal position; this is often found in patients who do not use articles. Perlmutter's hypothesis (1970) that *a* is the reduced form of *one* may be invoked in this connection. With the exception of one isolated utterance of 'I', no pronouns were produced by the subject; in referring to himself, the patient would use his full name.

A less severely impaired subject—who sometimes but not always omits copulas, sentence subjects, and determiners—is described by Schnitzer (1974). Schnitzer's analysis indicates that these structures fail to appear overtly only when the information they would have contained is redundant; that is, when the 'context of situation', the preceding discourse, or the features of the current utterance uniquely (more or less!) determine the form of the copula, subject, or determiner, then that element may fail to be expressed. Pronouns are sometimes used by this patient, e.g. 'He mad', 'They not fast', but in other cases it is not uncommon to find the antecedent noun phrase being repeated in contexts where a normal subject would use an anaphoric pronoun (Goodglass *et al.*, 1972). These patterns again suggest that the deficit in agrammatism is 'constructional' rather than phonological or articulatory.

In summary, much of the data on agrammatism can be interpreted in terms of four principles: (1) The (surface) structure of utterances is elaborated from top to bottom (as suggested by Fodor *et al.*, 1974); (2) Lexical insertion may take place at too high a level in the tree; (3) The lexicon is itself biased (Marshall and Newcombe, 1966; Marshall and Holmes, 1974)—nouns are easier to access than any other part of speech (and will be found playing the roles of subject, object, and adverbials of time and place); (4) Computational complexity is cumulative in the sense that the 'functional load' imposed by choices made on semantic and syntactic levels determines, in part, whether or not an element will enter the articulatory program; hence parts of speech that are not expressed in 'propositional' utterances may be expressed in 'automatic' language.

To a first approximation, then, agrammatic patients speak 'ein *korrekter* Telegrammstil' (Isserlin, 1922) and the temptation to regard the *basic* symptomology as a relatively peripheral 'expressive' difficulty should probably be resisted; elements are not 'deleted' before the articulatory program is run, they were never there in the first place. The notion that agrammatism is not solely an 'output' difficulty (in some patients at least) would seem to be needed in order to understand how in Zurif *et al*.'s data (1972) there is such a striking parallelism between the speech-characteristics of the subjects and their performance on a linguistic judgement task which requires no overtly spoken response. What we are seeing in agrammatism is the obligatory (and exaggerated) use of a perfectly normal, albeit optional, strategy. It would be pedantic to respond to the question, 'Where are you going?' with the utterance 'I am going home.' 'Home' suffices, and there is no reason to assume that a surface tree corresponding to the full reply was ever formulated.

Let us now contrast the syndrome of agrammatism with a condition that is in many ways its polar opposite.

PROPOSITIONS WITHOUT PARTICULARS

A patient seen by Newcombe and Smith (1970) is asked to describe a complex, representational picture which is placed in front of him; part of the transcript reads as follows:

That's the . . . you know, the . . . very much like they got on the . . . on something very much. I don't say that it's the proper one but it's like er er . . . I can't say it but I can just . . . yes, that could be it, could be a bit like that, yes. No, I wasn't thinking of that one, not at that time. I wasn't, no.

This subject shows a sophisticated ability to control sentence structure, including relative clause formation, conjunction with *but*, modals, articles, pronouns, and prepositional phrases. The striking loss of specific lexical items (nouns, adjectives, and verbs) and their 'replacement' by indefinites ('something') and pronouns ('one', 'it') results, however, in a discourse the informativeness of which is essentially zero.

Goodglass (1968) provides part of another transcript which is typical of the condition; the patient has been asked why he is in hospital:

Well, I had trouble with . . . oh, almost everything that happened from the . . . eh, eh . . . Golly, the word I can remember, you know, is ah . . . When I had the . . . ah biggest . . . ah . . . that I had the trouble with, and I still have a . . . the . . . ah . . . different . . . The things I want to say . . .

ah . . . The way I say things, but I understand mostly things, most of them, and what they are.

Again there is no lack of complex coordinate and subordinate constructions; forms are used fluently and paraphrased with facility, but the patient has demonstrated, not described, his disability. 'Failure of explicit communication' (Wepman and Jones, 1964) and considerable repetitiveness is also illustrated in Wepman and Jones' example of the syndrome. The patient is asked to describe her family; she replies:

Yes! we . . . when I know. If I know that they're good, they're wonderful. Why don't I say what we have, because we have everything. But good, they're good. They are good to me.

In clinical taxonomies of the aphasias, the above patients would be labelled as suffering from amnesic aphasia (Goldstein, 1948) or anomia (Kleist, 1934) or nominal aphasia (Head, 1926) or verbal amnesia (Brown, 1972) or semantic aphasia (Wepman and Jones, 1964). I shall in general regard these terms as synonymous; proliferation of terminology is characteristic of the field. Yet each label does carry a certain 'excess of meaning' which conveys implicitly, a theoretical attitude towards the disorder. A fairly clear account of the signs, both positive and negative, which define the condition can, however, be extracted from the writings of workers whose interpretations may differ markedly.

Anomia is one of the 'fluent' aphasias in the sense that phrase length and rate of speech are within normal bounds (if we ignore the word-finding gaps); appropriate intonation contours are preserved and there is little suggestion of articulatory difficulties, although phonological and semantic paraphasias *may* be in evidence. Comprehension and repetition of verbal material may be well-preserved; difficulties with confrontation naming (in all sensory modalities) are pronounced. The picture, then, is of a patient who can construct quite elaborate surface trees and who can handle the syntactic trappings of the language; the deficit seems to lie at the level of lexical insertion, implicating semantic and/or phonological matrices.

Can this description be made a little more precise? As the terms 'anomia' and 'nominal aphasia' imply, early workers were of the opinion that nouns were more likely to be unavailable than any other part-of-speech. Thus Broadbent (1884) describes a case who '. . . was scarcely ever known to utter a noun substantive, and if he did, it was so to speak, inadvertently and erroneously'. The deficit was selective, for Broadbent continues: 'Other words he said unhesitatingly, and he would employ fairly long phrases, speaking them smoothly and naturally so long as a noun did not come in his way.' Broadbent reports by way of example such utterances as 'I am very glad to see you', 'I am very much better today, thank you', 'I cannot remember it at all.' When asking for something, the patient would use such expressions as 'I want the one' or 'Please give me the one.'

It is interesting to note in this context that Bach (1968) derives noun phrases from underlying structures of the form *Determiner + one + S*; elements which appear as nouns in surface structure are held to arise from relative clauses based on a predicate nominal constituent developed from the S node. In a somewhat similar fashion, Postal (1966) derives pronouns from underlying structures of the form:

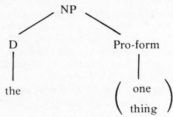

This latter analysis has not however met with universal support (Dougherty, 1974).

Reports of cases in which it is claimed that 'memory is good for all parts of speech except noun-substantives and proper names' (Graves, 1851) are extremely common (Bastian, 1887; Lichtheim, 1885; Jacobi, 1887; Kussmaul, 1885); and it has been suggested that in all forms of 'fluent' aphasia (anomia, Wernicke's aphasia, jargon aphasia) nouns are the most severely impaired category. Thus Ross (1885) remarks: 'The loss of the noun is the most marked feature of sensory (Wernicke's: JCM) aphasia.' Goodglass (1968), stressing the contrasts between non-fluent and fluent aphasias, writes: 'One variable, however, that can be stated only in linguistic terms is that of nominal or substantive function—a quality that facilitates speech production for the agrammatic but that inhibits it for the fluent aphasic.' This claim is echoed in the studies of jargon aphasia reported by Buckingham and Kertesz (1974).

Yet in other cases (with an overall pattern of loss and retention of linguistic abilities that is characteristic of classical anomia) it is reported that the deficit is equally severe for all major lexical classes, nouns, adjectives and verbs. The patients reported by Goldstein (1906) and Goldstein and Gelb (1924) illustrate this pattern; in the first case Goldstein notes that whilst the patient frequently used 'Ding' (thing) where a specific noun would have been appropriate, it was if anything even more common for her to express all activities by using 'überfahren' (a dialect form of 'ausfuehren' = 'perform').

Are there, then, two subtypes of word-finding difficulty in the fluent aphasias, or is it rather the case that systematic errors of observation have entered the literature? The latter position is taken by Elder (1897) and expounded (with considerable supporting data) by Wepman, Bock, Jones and Van Pelt (1956). They state: '. . . anomia may be characterized by the loss of all but the most general (and hence most frequent) words in the language.' We can illustrate their position by the following stratagem. Consider this 'protocol' of an 'aphasic patient's' spontaneous speech:

I have one or more of them. It's a . . . I like them. It must be over there in the . . . by the . . . but it's not. My . . . also made one for some . . . that he had been with in the . . . as a . . . it was before he had his . . . most of them are like that. They can also be had from the . . . a man has them, many of them, but a new one would be even more of a . . . Did you have one when you were with them? You said that you had one from the time that you were at . . . No, if that were so, you could not have made so much . . . at it all these years. Even then it's not the first new one that I must have been through.

The 'protocol' is reasonably grammatical, save for the 'anomic gaps'; the most salient feature of the 'extract' is the 'patient's' inability to produce *specific* noun phrases. A few nouns (*time, man, years*) are uttered but certainly the deficit seems to be disproportionately severe for nouns.

The catch, of course, is that I have made up this passage from the 100 most frequent words in the language (Kučera and Francis, 1967). The above three nouns are the *only* nouns which occur in this subset (at rank orders 67, 81 and 95 respectively). We have ample evidence (Howes and Geschwind, 1964; Oldfield, 1966) that a dramatic shift in the word-frequency distribution occurs in many patients after aphasia-producing injuries; the ability to utter and comprehend words which are rare in the language is disproportionately affected relative to performance with more common words. The *appearance* of a noun-deficit could be no more than a reflection of the way in which members of particular syntactic classes are distributed in the word-frequency statistics. The issue of whether the fluent aphasias are characterized by a selective reduction in the availability of nouns or in the availability of low-frequency words should accordingly be regarded as an open question. It is also worth noting that the causal status of 'relative frequency of occurrence' is itself subject to doubt. The psychological efficacy of frequency variation may be due to the high correlation of frequency with age-of-acquisition (Carroll and White, 1973); alternatively (or in addition), the notion of relative generality (characterized perhaps in terms of number of semantic features) may be the operative factor, with frequency again being a correlated but non-causal variable (Werner, 1956).

Considerations of specificity lead back to the question of whether the anomic deficit should be regarded as an impairment of phonological or of semantic 'memory'. Let us see how a typical 'memory' interpretation ('amnesic aphasia') is formulated. Bateman (1892, Case 1) provides an excellent case report. Initially, the patient's 'cerebral congestion' led to a 'complete but temporary loss of speech'; the sole utterance which remained to him was 'Oh dear, Oh dear'. Within a month, however, considerable restitution of function has taken place and the patient displays a classical 'verbal amnesia'.

He understands all that is said, but is affected with an incapacity to employ substantives, having lost the memory of words as far as that part of speech is concerned, and he will make use of a periphrase to avoid using the substantive required. He has very clear ideas as to what he wishes to say, is aware that he is wrong in the use of words, is vexed at his blunders, and is ingenious in contriving means to counteract or avoid them. If asked to fetch an object, he will bring the right, but if he wants anyone else to fetch or give him anything, he more commonly asks for the wrong thing first, afterwards correcting himself, showing that he understands perfectly what he wants. If shown anything, he will say that he knows what it is, but cannot say it. On being shown a purse, and being asked what it was, he answered, 'I can't say the word; I know what it is; it is to put money in.' 'Is it a knife?' 'No.' 'An umbrella?' 'No.' 'A purse?' 'Yes.' I showed him a poker. 'What is it?' 'I know, but I cannot say the word.' 'What is its use?' 'To make up the fire.' 'Is it a walking stick?' 'No.' 'Is it a broom?' 'No.' 'Is it a poker?' 'Yes,' he said instantly, with a smile evincing complete understanding of the question, and joy at the certainty that he had answered it right. It was evident, therefore, that the words representing his ideas were preserved in the treasury of his memory, but the mere origination of the ideas was not sufficient to effect the verbal expression of them.

Superficially, it would seem that the locus of such 'retrieval' failures *must* be phonological. Patients can demonstrate (by circumlocation and paraphrase) that they know what they want to say; they can 'recognize' the word they are seeking as witness their acceptance of the correct word when prompted by the examiner (Goldstein, 1906). The word is then promptly 'forgotten' again.

On showing him a tumbler glass he shakes his head, and says it is for beer, but cannot remember its name; he knows it is not called a basin, a mug, or a jug, and recognises the word 'glass' directly it is named; but the next minute he has forgotten it, and cannot repeat it. (Bateman, 1892)

We might argue, then, that spontaneous utterances are elaborated to the point where surface trees with full semantic specification are available:

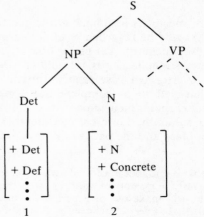

But, in the course of 'reading out' this specification from left-to-right, the patient finds that he cannot retrieve the phonological matrix which corresponds to the semantic specifications of nouns and/or low frequency words irrespective of syntactic class.

One would expect in such a phonological 'tip-of-the-tongue' state that the less-severely affected patient might be able to provide some information about the overt form of the 'missing' response. Features such as the initial phone, the number of syllables in the word, and the placement of primary stress might be recalled when the word as a whole is unavailable. There is evidence that this is so in some cases of both normal and aphasic subjects (Woodworth, 1938; Brown and McNeill, 1966; Yarmey, 1973; Baker, 1974; Barton, 1971).

An interesting aphasic case is reported by Graves (1851) who regards the condition as '. . . a remarkably exaggerated degree of the common defect of memory observed in the diseases of old age . . .' His patient

. . . perfectly recollected the initial letter of every substantive or proper name for which he had occasion in conversation, though he could not recall to his memory the word itself. Experience had taught him the utility of having written on manuscript a list of the things he was in the habit of calling for or speaking about, including the proper names of his children, servants, and acquaintances: all these he arranged alphabetically in a little pocket dictionary, which he used as follows: if he wished to ask anything about a cow, before he commenced the sentence he turned to the letter C, and looked out the word 'cow' and kept his finger and eye fixed on the word until he had finished the sentence. He could pronounce the word 'cow' in its proper place so long as he had his eyes fixed upon the written letters; but the moment he shut his book it passed out of his memory and could not be recalled . . .

The patient could not remember his own name; this was likewise inscribed in his pocketbook.

Some patients spontaneously cue themselves by writing the word on paper or tracing it in the air (see Grashey, 1855, and Case W. L. in Whitaker, 1971) but this is probably rare in aphasia (and in normal subjects?).

'Anomic' gaps may, then, reflect partial or total failure to access phonological (and/or graphemic) structure, given semantic representations which are fully-specified at the word level. Meaning—form correspondences are, of course, largely arbitrary in natural languages; so-called 'phonetic symbolism', if it exists at all, plays a very minor role in marking semantically related words. The very capriciousness of the association between form and content could make access to phonological structure peculiarly liable to failure and error.

But it is by no means certain that locating the deficit at the level of association between 'word' (in the sense of 'content') and 'form' is the only possibility. Consider an ordinary monolingual dictionary (recently discovered by generative semanticists). It will contain such information as *prolific* = producing many offspring; *prolong* = cause to last longer; *promontory* = point of high land jutting out to sea (Penguin English Dictionary, revised edition, 1969). Each 'word' in each definition (= brief explanation of the meaning of a word or phrase) will, in turn, be further decomposable, e.g. *sea* = large expanse of salt water. The point is that semantic structures, however formalized (Katz, 1967; Bierwisch, 1969; McCawley, 1971), are not to be *identified* with words. Rather, semantic structures can be 'lexicalized' in a variety of ways, and the particular lexicalization chosen determines the overt form, a form which can be articulated. One could, then, consider the possibility that anomia might be a disorder of lexicalization rather than of phonological retrieval.

Katz (1966) gives the following 'dictionary entry' for *chase*: Verb Transitive, . . .; (((Activity) (Nature: (Physical)) of X), (Movement) (Rate: Fast)) Character: Following)), (Intention of X: (Trying to catch ((y) ((Movement) (Rate: Fast)))); <SR>. This reading is intended to capture the sense of *chase* in, e.g., 'The policemen *chase* the criminals'. But presumably a paraphrase of the sentence (or at least a good approximation to it) would be: 'The policemen quickly follow the criminals with the intention of trying to catch them.' In other words, it is not necessary that Katz's dictionary entries be realized monolexemically (although there may be a constraint upon normal communication to the effect of 'Do not say in ten words what you can say in one'—except when talking to children or foreigners. This would be a 'conversational maxim' in Grice's sense, 1967).

We could think of lexicalization—in the context of a language-production model—as the transcription of semantic features into dummy place holders in order to achieve representations which are realizable by one (or more) word(s). 'Word' would here mean 'element specified in a form such that a phonological representation may be associated with it'. Semantic structures do not and should not provide a level of description at which phonological information can be stated.

Anomic deficits could, then, be interpreted as a (partial) failure of transcription from the semantic code into 'words'. Imagine that such transcription takes place at a much reduced rate in the fluent aphasias, an effect analogous perhaps to the known reduction in the rate of short-term memory scanning in aphasia (Swinney and Taylor, 1971). From a semantic representation which could be realized as 'The policemen chase the criminals', the anomic subject 'blocks' on *chase*; *ex hypothesi*, by the time that the noun phrase object is activated (i.e. is seeking access to lexicalization) only the first semantic feature following the word boundary after *policemen*

has been read into the place holder, $\begin{bmatrix} +\text{Verb Trans} \\ +\text{Activity} \end{bmatrix}$, the place holder is closed (i.e. a right-hand bracket is assigned), and the process continues. A procedure of this nature would result in fluent speech (without overt 'word-finding' pauses) which was relatively content-less; overt blocking would ensue if a sequence of semantic features which did not have a monolexemic realization in the language was read into the dummy, e.g. (+ Activity, + Physical; + Movement; + Fast; + Following). That is, there is no single word in English (although there may be in some other language) which means 'to follow quickly'. In these circumstances, an overt hesitation pause will ensue; the patient may try again, perhaps producing a circum-locution, that is, a sequence of place markers each of which contains a proper subset of the semantic features in the conceptual code.

Much the same argument can be made within the framework of lexicalization adopted by proponents of generative semantics. Thus McCawley (1968) suggests that a structure of the (approximate) form:

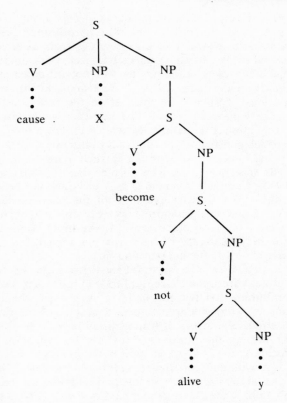

underlies the overt sentence 'X killed Y'. By the (optional) rule of predicate-raising, V nodes can be daughter-adjointed to the right of the next-highest V. This process *creates* constituents which can be replaced by lexical items (but see Fodor, 1970), i.e. can be associated with a phonological shape. It does not make sense to ask of McCawley's base representation for *kill* such a question as 'How many syllables does the item have?'. If the relevant constituent is not created the issue can never arise. Similarly, to return to my 'psychologization' of Katz' model, the patient cannot have access to *any* phonological information about the 'missing word' *chase*. The 'word' *chase* was never created in the first place and therefore cannot 'go missing'.

The above arguments indicate (albeit in a very preliminary fashion) the *possibility* of an alternative to the assumption that fluent anomic aphasias must be characterized as failure to retrieve phonological form. The notion of mapping from conceptual semantics to 'word' semantics would also permit one to regard the verbal paraphasias characteristic of fluent aphasia as errors at the level of lexical transcription. A normal subject is not immune from making such mistakes, although he will not infrequently correct them, e.g. (from Fromkin, 1973): 'There are a lot of answers—I mean questions', 'When were you last on the west—east coast?', 'I would have gone—come . . .' The fact that a mismatch is perceived clearly implies the continued availability of a level of representation which marks the 'correct' (that is, intended) form.

The aphasic patient who produces such paraphasic errors in spontaneous speech *may* likewise correct them (Saint-Paul, 1904; Piéron, 1923). Case 1 of Bateman (1892) and Case 4 of Elder (1897) illustrate this point; further examples of the phenomenon, taken from confrontation object-naming tasks, are provided in Newcombe and Marshall (1972). In other cases, for example, Stengel (1933), the patient may be aware of his error but repeated attempts at correction lead only to further paraphasias.

Transcription, then, can fail in (at least) two ways. Features may be read correctly from the conceptual code to the 'word' level, but in groups containing too few members or in groups which are not proper subsets of the code with respect to language-specific lexicalization; alternatively, errors of transcription may arise which nonetheless do respect the notion of 'possible lexicalization'. In the former instance, the content of speech will be vague and circumlocutory but will not contain semantic paraphasias (Goldstein, 1906); in the latter, the pattern of loss and retention will be reversed (Bateman, 1892, Case 2). In neither case is it *necessary* to postulate that access to phonological information is impaired.

FROM LANGUAGE TO SPEECH

The construction of a full surface tree—that is, a syntactic object containing semantically appropriate lexical entries—is not the terminal point of linguistic communication; these central computations must link to an output device (the vocal tract), the configurations of which produce physical perturbations of the environment when air is forced through the system. Neuromotor commands must trigger the speech-producing musculature. A wide variety of models have been proposed which attempt to specify the order of computation of the putative interlevels (e.g. syllabic, phonemic, allophonic) which mediate between syntax and motor command (see Fromkin, 1968; Laver, 1970); considerable attention has also been paid to the nature of the closed-loop feedback from the periphery which enables relatively invariant 'phonetic targets' to be realized via quite different movements of the articulators in space and time (MacNeilage, 1970; Sussman, 1972).

Although disorders of *speech* production are not a necessary component of the syndromes of aphasia, they are found in the majority of patients. Illustrative examples of articulatory and phonic distortions can be found in Shankweiler and Harris (1966) where it is shown that in patients with so-called 'phonetic disintegration' fricatives, affricates and linked consonant groups are especially difficult to produce. Individual case studies of two, quite distinct symptom-complexes—'motor aphasia' and 'jargon aphasia' have demonstrated systematic errors of *place* and *manner* of articulation, with *place* errors pre-dominating (Fry, 1959; Green, 1969). The patient reported by Fry also made many errors of voicing in which, particularly with plosives, a voiced consonant was more likely to be replaced by a voiceless consonant (e.g. /g/ → /k/) than vice versa. Simplifications of sound structure are also seen in Green's patient whose errors show that 'the feature of nasality is more likely to be lost than gained'. I shall not discuss such impairment in any detail here but simply note that some success has been reported in distinguishing between phonological and phonetic disorders, and that the former seem susceptible to insightful analysis in terms of distinctive feature notation and markedness theory (Blumstein, 1973). In distinguishing between aphasic disorders of speech production and the dysarthrias, as seen in bulbar and pseudobulbar palsy, the variability in pronounciation from occasion to occasion is perhaps the most striking feature which is observed after cortical injury. Data (and further references) relevant to the analysis of phonic impairment can be found in Johns and Darley (1970), Lecours and Lhermitte (1969) and Alajouanine, Ombredane, and Durand (1939).

Although a number of phonologic levels mediate between syntax and output, it seems likely (as in the case of the agrammatic patient) that the 'computational load' of semantic and syntactic elaboration is carried over into the phonological component. Thus Green (1969) reports on a case of Wernicke's aphasia (with copious jargon) whose spontaneous speech manifests neologisms (and semantically inappropriate words) the occurrence of which appears to be syntactically conditioned. Green claims that '. . . neologisms generally occur in the predicate of a sentence' and he provides data to show that when the grammatical status of a neologism can be judged (on the basis of the well-formed parts of the utterance) there is a 5·5 to 1 ratio of 'nouns' to 'verbs'. A qualitatively similar pattern is reported in Buckingham and Kertesz (1974, Case B.F.);

they suggest that neologisms and paraphasias '. . . are quite often anticipatory or perseverative in nature and frequently arise during anomic gaps in the stream of speech'. It is consistent with this position that the course of remission in Green's patient progressed from jargon aphasia to classical anomia with indefinite noun phrases such as 'somebody', 'that' and 'it' greatly in evidence. Sentences such as 'She started to do something, I would tell her not to do it, you know' were produced in contexts where neither deictic nor anaphoric factors permitted the referants of the noun phrases to be known.

Anticipatory and perseverative errors draw attention to the general problem of achieving temporal synchrony between a (partially) top-to-bottom process (the elaboration of structural descriptions) and a strictly left-to-right process (the sequential production of speech, or written language). The speech errors of normal subjects illustrate in a particularly clear fashion the effects of failure to synchronize levels in the production process. Lexicalization and surface syntax may get 'out of step'; Bolinger (1961) reports such examples as 'You have at your avail . . .' (= You have at your command/disposal + You have available), 'At base . . .' (= At bottom + Basically). Blends in which two semantically similar lexicalizations enter the phonological program within a single 'word' slot are common; close/near → 'clear', best/most → 'boast', transposed/transcribed → 'transpised', dealer/salesman → 'dealsman', survey/review → 'surview' (Fromkin, 1973). Overt anticipations, perseverations, and reversals indicate that elements may enter the phonological code in misplaced sequence; A Canadian from Toronto → 'A Tanadian . . .', black boxes → 'black bloxes', left hemisphere → 'heft lemisphere' (Fromkin, 1973). Simple phonemic paraphasias in subjects with brain injury are indistinguishable from the 'tips of the slung' made by normal subjects. Episodes of neologistic jargon—characterized by alliteration, assonance and other reduplicative stereotypic patterns (Green, 1969; Buckingham and Kertesz, 1974)—would appear to differ only in degree; the basic phonological system of the speaker's language is respected (Lecours and Lhermitte, 1969).

A STOPPING MECHANISM?

We have so far considered the aphasias basically in terms of the 'loss' or unavailability of linguistic elements; but the verbal perseverations which are characteristic of many patients' speech represent in some sense an opposite problem. Elements are 'too available'; once activated they persist (Allison and Hurwitz, 1967). Extreme examples may be found after severe closed head injury. Thus Locke, Caplan and Kellar's (1973) Case 7 shows considerable palilalia in addition to dysarthric and phonological difficulties (although his comprehension of language is good):

I gull like smokin a teegarette. Oh no, I can, I got tigarette, I got tigarette. I, Oh, Oh, I got tigarette, I got tigarette, I got tigarette, I got tigarette. Gotta match, ya, gotta match, ya gotta match, ya gotta match, please. Ya gotta match, please, gotta match, please. I got cigarette. I—I got cigarette, I got tigarette . . . I didunt know I had em, I didunt know I had em, I didunt know I had em, I didunt know I had em . . .

Although the patient's rate of speech is quite fast (182 words per minute), the amount of information conveyed per unit time is clearly low. The metaphor of a stuck gramophone needle is *not* appropriate for the palilalia is restricted to phrases and sentences. This regularity—palilalia respects the integrity of linguistic units, words, phrases and sentences—is also characteristic of the repetitions found in the speech of patients with Parkinson's disease, the most frequent 'cause' of palilalia. During the reiterations in Parkinsonism '. . . speech tends to be uttered more and more quickly and with less distinctness, so that the latter part may be almost inaudible' (Critchley, 1927). Loudness also diminishes during the course of the reiterations. The patient is usually '. . . fully aware of his defect but cannot as a rule control it' (Critchley, 1927). In some cases (e.g. Marie and Levy, 1925) the palilalia, whilst pronounced in spontaneous speech, does not appear during 'automatic' or 'serial speech'. Marie's patient, where the palilalia was of encephalic origin, did not show iterations while counting from one to twenty, listing the letters of the alphabet, or singing. In other cases, however, palilalia may affect spontaneous speech, responding to questions and emotional speech. Critchley's Case 1 (1927), again a postencephalitic patient, was palilalic in a wide variety of circumstances:

Whilst at the cinema he found himself reading aloud *over and over again* the captions of the films; his wife, getting annoyed, dug him in the ribs and said 'For God's sake, Bob, shut up,' but all the patient could reply was 'I can't shut up, I can't shut up, I can't shut up, I can't shut up.'

The palilalia persisted even when swearing! In Critchley's Case 4, however, with 'a very gross palilia which was constantly present during conversation', there were 'no repetitions when he counted aloud, and none when he swore in anger'.

Whatever the constraints on palilalia in terms of the type of language being produced, I know of no example where linguistic units are violated by the process. This is further evidence that surface structure trees are implicated in the language production process; that is, possible iterations are controlled by nodes in the syntactic description of sentences:

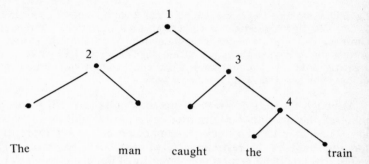

Palilalia may thus produce:

The man caught the train, the man caught the train (iteration on 1)
The man, the man, the man caught the train (iteration on 2)
The man caught the train, caught the train (iteration on 3)
The man caught the train, the train (iteration on 4)

The condition does *not* produce:

* The man caught, man caught, man caught the train.
* The man caught the, caught the, caught the train.
* The man caught the, man caught the, man caught the train.

'Pure' palilalia may sometimes coexist with what could be called 'expanded' or 'semantic' palilalia. Thus Brown (1972) notes that 'At times, the repetition is incorporated into a following statement, tending to obscure its reiterative character, as in "I used to work, for a time I used to work as a painter".' A patient with Parkinson's disease that I once saw produced pure iterations of words:

'Yes, to Churnside, Churnside, Churnside',

of phrases:

'My sister, my sister, my sister had a holiday in Sweden',

and of sentences:

'It's just dune the road, it's just dune the road, it's just dune the road, it's just dune the road'.

In addition, however, a node would frequently be 'expanded' during a palilalic episode: e.g.

My sister, my sister had a holiday in Sweden. My sister, my sister, had a lovely holiday in Sweden.
They're getting big, you know, they're getting big now, you know.

Occasionally, semantic substitutions would enter:

He got two or three medals, got two or three medals, got two or three medals, got two or three medals. He didn't work for the big team, big team, he worked for the junior team, he didn't work for the big team, he played for the junior team, he played for the junior club.

In these latter examples, the patient must be 'returning' to the deeper representation which guided the construction of the surface structure tree.

Palilalia is often found in the context of other perseverative disorders, particularly the festinating gait which may be seen in Parkinsonism. Critchley (1970) mentions a patient (with post-encephalitic Parkinsonism) with severe palilalia who '. . . also tended to continue unduly with any repetitive act such as hammering a nail, combing his hair or brushing his teeth'. It has also been noted that 'many of these patients exhibit a variety of mutism alternating with their palilalia, as though loath to embark upon the act of speaking' (Critchley, 1927); this difficulty in initiating speech acts is again characteristic of the performance of other motor skills in Parkinsonism. The palilalic syndrome is not, then, a disorder of language (or speech) *per se,* but it does illustrate that, like other actions, speech must both start and stop.

Alajouanine, T. (1956). Verbal realization in aphasia. *Brain*, **79**, 1-28.

Alajouanine, T., Ombredane, A. and Durand, M. (1939). *Le syndrome de désintégration phonétique dans l'aphasie.* Paris: Masson and Cie.

Allison, R. S. and Hurwitz, L. J. (1967). On perseveration in aphasics. *Brain*, **90**, 429-48.

Bach, E. (1968). Nouns and noun phrases. In Bach, E. and Harms, R. T. (Eds.), *Universals in linguistic theory.* New York: Holt, Rinehart and Winston.

Baker, L. (1974). The lexicon: some psycholinguistic evidence. *UCLA Working Papers in Phonetics*, **26**, 1-132.

Banerji, R. B. (1963). Phrase structure languages, finite machines, and channel capacity. *Information and Control*, **6**, 153-62.

Barton, M. I. (1971). Recall of generic properties of words in aphasic patients. *Cortex*, **7**, 73-82.

Bastian, H. C. (1887). On different kinds of aphasia with special reference to their classification and ultimate pathology. *British Medical Journal*, 2, 931-6, 985-90.

Bastian, H. C. (1897). Some problems in connexion with aphasia and other speech defects. *Lancet*, 1, 933-42, 1005-17, 1131-7, 1187-94.

Bateman, F. (1892). On *aphasia, or loss of speech and the localization of the faculty of articulate language*. London: Churchill.

Bierwisch, M. (1969). Certain problems of semantic representation. *Foundation of Language*, 5, 153-84.

Blumstein, S. (1973). *A phonological investigation of aphasic speech*. The Hague: Mouton.

Bolinger, D. L. (1961). *Generality, gradience and the all-or-none*. The Hague: Mouton.

Botez, M. I. (1962). The starting mechanism of speech. *Proceedings of the 8th Congress of the Hungarian Neurologists and Psychiatrists*. Budapest.

Braine, M. D. S. (1974). Length constraints, reduction rules and holophrastic processes in children's word combinations. *Journal of Verbal Learning and Verbal Behavior*, 13, 448-56.

Broadbent, W. H. (1884). On a particular form of amnesia (loss of nouns). *Medico-Chirurgical Transactions*, 49, 249-64.

Broca, P. (1861). Remarques sur le Siége de la Faculté du Langage Articulé. *Bulletin de la Société d'Antomie*, 5, 330-57.

Brown, J. W. (1972). *Aphasia, apraxia, and agnosia*. Springfield, Illinois: C. C. Thomas.

Brown, R. and McNeill, D. (1966). The 'tip of the tongue' phenomenon. *Journal of Verbal Learning and Verbal Behavior*, 5, 325-37.

Buckingham, H. W. and Kertesz, A. (1974). A linguistic analysis of fluent aphasia. *Brain and Language*, 1, 43-62.

Cairns, H., Oldfield, R. C., Pennybacker, J. B. and Whitteridge, D. (1941). Akinetic mutism with an epidermoid cyst of the 3rd ventricle. *Brain*, 64, 273-90.

Caplan, D. and Marshall, J. C. (1975). Generative grammar and aphasic disorders: a theory of language representation in the human brain (Review article). *Foundations of Language*, 12, 583-96.

Carroll, J. B. and White, M. N. (1973). Word frequency and age of acquisition as determiners of picture naming latency. *Quarterly Journal of Experimental Psychology*, 25, 85-95.

Chomsky, N. (1957). *Syntactic structure*. The Hague: Mouton.

Chomsky, N. (1965). *Aspects of the theory of syntax*. Cambridge, Mass.: MIT Press.

Cohen, D. and Hécaen, H. (1965). Remarques neurolinguistiques sur un cas d'agrammatisme. *Journal de Psychologie normale et pathologique*, 62, 273-96.

Critchley, M. (1927). On palilalia. *Journal of Neurology*, 8, 23-32.

Critchley, M. (1970). *Aphasiology*. London: Arnold.

Dercum, F. X. (1894). A case of hemiplegia. *Journal of Nervous and Mental Disorders*, 21, 609-13.

De Villiers, J. (1974). Quantitative aspects of agrammatism in aphasia. *Cortex*, 10, 36-54.

Dougherty, R. C. (1974). What explanation is and isn't. In Cohen, D. (Ed.), *Explaining Linguistic Phenomena*. New York: Wiley.

Eccles, J. C. (1973). The cerebellum as a computer: patterns in space and time. *Journal of Physiology*, 228, 1-32.

Elder, W. (1897). *Aphasia and the cerebral speech mechanism*. London: H. K. Lewis.

Fillmore, C. J. (1968). The case for case. In Bach, E. and Harms, R. T. (Eds.), *Universals in linguistic theory*. New York: Holt, Rinehart and Winston.

Fodor, J. A. (1970). Three reasons for not deriving 'kill' from 'cause to die'. *Linguistic Inquiry*, 1, 429-38.

Fodor, J. A., Bever, T. G. and Garrett, M. F. (1974). *The psychology of language*. New York: McGraw-Hill.

Fromkin, V. (1968). Speculations on performance models. *Journal of Linguistics*, 4, 1-152.

Fromkin, V. (Ed.) (1973). *Speech errors as linguistic evidence*. The Hague: Mouton.

Fry, D. B. (1959). Phonemic substitutions in an aphasic patient. *Language and Speech*, 2, 52-61.

Geschwind, N. (1964). Non-aphasic disorders of speech. *International Journal of Neurology*, 4, 207-14.

Geschwind, N. and Howes, D. (1962). Statistical properties of aphasic language. MIT Mimeo.

Goldstein, K. (1906). Zur Frage der amnestischen Aphasie. *Archiv für Psychiatrie und Neurologie*, 41, 911-50.

Goldstein, K. (1948). *Language and language disturbances*. New York: Grune and Stratton.

Goldstein, K. and Gelb, A. (1924). Über Farbeamnesie. *Psychologische Forschung*, 6, 127-86.

Goodglass, H. (1968). Studies on the grammar of aphasics. In Rosenberg, S. and Koplin, J. (Eds.), *Developments in applied psycholinguistic research*. New York: Macmillan.

Goodglass, H. and Berko, J. (1960). Agrammatism and inflectional morphology in English. *Journal of Speech and Hearing Research*, 3, 257-67.

Goodglass, H., Gleason, J. B., Bernholz, N. A. and Hyde, M. R. (1972). Some linguistic structures in the speech of a Broca's aphasic. *Cortex*, 8, 191-212.

Goodglass, H., Quadfasel, F. and Timberlake, W. (1964). Phrase length and the type and severity of aphasia. *Cortex*, 1, 133-53.

Grashey, H. (1885). Über Aphasie und ihre Beziehungen zur Wahrnehmung. *Archiv für Psychiatrie*, 16, 654-88.

Graves, R. J. (1851). Singular defect and impotence of memory after paralysis. *Dublin Quarterly Journal of Medical Science*, 11, 1-4.

Green, E. (1969). Phonological and grammatical aspects of jargon in an aphasic patient. *Language and Speech*, 12, 103-18.

Grice, H. P. (1967). Logic and conversation. Mimeo version of the William James Lectures.

Head, H. (1926). *Aphasia and kindred disorders of speech.* New York: Macmillan.

Howes, D. and Geschwind, N. (1964). Quantitative studies of aphasic language. In Rioch, D. M. and Weinstein, E. A. (Eds.), *Disorders of communication.* Baltimore: Williams and Wilkins.

Isserlin, M. (1922). Ueber Agrammatismus. *Zeitschrift für die gesamte Neurologie und Psychiatrie*, 75, 332-410.

Jackson, J. H. (1874). On the nature of the duality of the brain. *Medical Press and Circular*, 1, 19-63.

Jackson, J. H. (1878). On affections of speech from disease of the brain. *Brain*, 1, 304-30.

Jacobi, M. P. (1887). Note on the special liability to loss of nouns in aphasia. *Journal of Nervous and Mental Disorders*, 14, 94-110.

Jacobs, R. A. and Rosenbaum, P. S. (1968). *English transformational grammar.* Waltham, Mass.: Ginn Blaisdell.

Jakobson, R. (1941). *Kindersprache, Aphasie und allgemeine Lautgesetze.* Uppsala: Universitets Arsskrift.

Jakobson, R. (1964). Towards a linguistic typology of aphasic impairments. In De Reuck, A. V. S. and O'Connor, M. (Eds.), *Disorders of language.* London: Churchill.

Johns, D. F. and Darley, F. L. (1970). Phonemic variability in apraxia of speech. *Journal of Speech and Hearing Research*, 13, 556-83.

Katz, J. (1966). *The philosophy of language.* New York: Harper and Row.

Katz, J. (1967). Recent issues in semantic theory. *Foundations of Language*, 3, 124-94.

Kleist, K. (1934). *Gehirnpathologie.* Leipzig: Barth.

Kučera, H. and Francis, W. N. (1967). *Computational analysis of present day English.* Providence, Rhode Island: Brown University Press.

Kussmaul, A. (1885). *Die Störungen der Sprache.* Leipzig: Vogel.

Labov, W. (1969). Contraction, deletion and inherent variability of the English Copula. *Language*, 45, 715-62.

Laver, J. (1970). The production of speech. In Lyons, J. (Ed.), *New horizons in linguistics.* Harmondsworth: Penguin Books.

Lecours, A. R. and Lhermitte, F. (1969). Phonemic paraphasias: linguistic structures and tentative hypotheses. *Cortex*, 5, 193-228.

Lichtheim, L. (1885). On aphasia. *Brain*, 7, 433-84.

Locke, S., Caplan, D. and Keller, L. (1973). *A study in neurolinguistics.* Springfield, Illinois: C. C. Thomas.

Luria, A. R. (1958). Brain disorders and language analysis. *Language and Speech*, 1, 14-34.

Marie, P. and Levy, G. (1925). Un singulier trouble de la parole: la palilalie. *Monde Medicale*, 35, 329-44.

Marshall, J. C. and Holmes, J. M. (1974). Sex, handedness and differential hemispheric specialization for components of word perception. *Journal of International Research Communications: Medical Science,* 2, 1344.

Marshall, J. C. and Newcombe, F. (1966). Syntactic and semantic errors in paralexia. *Neuropsychologia*, 4, 169-76.

Marshall, M., Newcombe, F. and Marshall, J. C. (1970). The microstructure of word-finding difficulties in a dysphasic patient. In Flores D'Arcais, G. B. and Levelt, W. J. M. (Eds.), *Advances in psycholinguistics*. Amsterdam: North-Holland.

MacNeilage, P. F. (1970). Motor control of serial ordering of speech. *Psychological Review*, 77, 182-96.

McCawley, J. D. (1968). The role of semantics in a grammar. In Bach, E. and Harms, R. T. (Eds.), *Universals in linguistic theory*. New York: Holt, Rinehart and Winston.

McCawley, J. D. (1971). Prelexical syntax. *Monograph series on Languages and Linguistics*, 24, 19-33.

Monrad-Krohn, G. H. (1947). Dysprosody or altered melody of language. *Brain*, 70, 405-15.

Myerson, R. and Goodglass, H. (1972). Transformational grammars of three agrammatic patients. *Language and Speech*, 15, 40-50.

Newcombe, F. and Marshall, J. C. (1972). Word retrieval in aphasia. *International Journal of Mental Health*, 1, 38-45.

Newcombe, F. and Smith, P. T. (1970). Personal communication.

Oldfield, R. C. (1966). Things, words and the brain. *Quarterly Journal of Experimental Psychology*, 18, 340-53.

Panse, F. and Shimoyama, T. (1955). Zur Auswirkung aphasischer Störungen im Japanischen: Agrammatismus und Paragrammatismus. *Archiv für Psychiatrie und Nervenkrankheiten*, 193, 131-8.

Perlmutter, D. (1970). On the article in English. In Bierwisch, M. and Heidolph, K. (Eds.), *Progress in Linguistics*. The Hague: Mouton.

Pick, A. (1913). *Die agrammatischen Sprachstörungen*. Berlin: Springer.

Pick, A. (1931). Aphasie. *Handbuch der normalen und pathologischen Physiologie*, 15, 1416-524.

Piéron, H. (1923). *Le Cerveau et la Pensée*. Paris: Alcan.

Postal, P. (1966). On so-called pronouns in English. *Monograph series on Languages and Linguistics*, 19, 176-206.

Rommel, P. (1683). De aphonia rara. *Miscellanea Curiosa Medico-Physica Academiae Naturae Curiosorum*, 2, 222-7.

Rosenblith, W. A. (1967). Discussion. In Millikan, C. H. and Darley, F. L. (Eds.), *Brain mechanisms underlying speech and language*. New York: Grune and Stratton.

Ross, J. (1885). *Handbook of the diseases of the nervous system*. Philadelphia: Lippincott.

Saint-Paul, G. (1904). *Le langage interieur et les paraphasies*. Paris: Alcan.

Salomon, E. (1914). Motorische Aphasie mit Agrammatismus und sensorischagrammatischen Stoerungen. *Monatsschrift für Psychiatrie und Neurologie*, 35, 181-208, 216-75.

Schnitzer, M. L. (1974). Aphasiological evidence for five linguistic hypotheses. *Language*, 50, 300-15.

Shankweiler, D. and Harris, K. S. (1966). An experimental approach to the problem of articulation in aphasia. *Cortex*, 2, 277-92.

Stengel, E. (1933). Zur Lehre von der Leitungsaphasie. *Zeitschrift für die gesamte Neurologie und Psychiatrie*, 149, 266-91.

Sussman, H. M. (1972). What the tongue tells the brain. *Psychological Bulletin*, 77, 262-72.

Swinney, D. A. and Taylor, O. L. (1971). Short-term memory recognition search in aphasics. *Journal of Speech and Hearing Research*, 14, 578-88.

Tissot, R., Mounin, G. and Lhermitte, F. (1973). *L'Agrammatisme*. Bruxelles: Dessart.

Traill, A. (1970). Transformational grammar and the case of an Ndebele speaking aphasic. *Journal of South African Logopedic Society*, 17, 48-66.

Van Lancker, D. (1975). Heterogeneity in language and speech: neurolinguistic studies. *UCLA Working Papers in Phonetics*, 29, 1-220.

Wepman, J. M. and Jones, L. V. (1964). Five aphasias: a commentary on aphasia as a regressive linguistic phenomenon. In Rioch, D. M. and Weinstein, E. A. (Eds.), *Disorders of communication*. Baltimore: Williams and Wilkins.

Wepman, J. M., Bock, R. D., Jones, L. V. and Van Pelt, D. (1956). Psycholinguistic study of aphasia: a revision of the concept of anomia. *Journal of Speech and Hearing Disorders*, 21, 468-77.

Werner, H. (1956). Microgenesis and aphasia. *Journal of Abnormal and Social Psychology*, 52, 347-53.

Whitaker, H. (1971). *On the representation of language in the human brain*. Edmonton: Linguistic Research.

Whitaker, H. (1972). Unsolicited nominalizations by aphasics: the plausibility of the lexicalist model. *Linguistics*, 78, 62-71.

Woodworth, R. S. (1938). *Experimental Psychology*. New York: Holt.

Yarmey, A. D. (1973). I recognize your face but I can't remember your name: further evidence on the tip-of-the-tongue phenomenon. *Memory and Cognition*, 1, 287-90.

Yngve, V. (1960). A model and an hypothesis for language structure. *Proceedings of the American Philosophical Society*, 104, 444-66.

Zurif, E. B., Caramazza, A. and Myerson, R. (1972). Grammatical judgments of agrammatic aphasics. *Neuropsychologia*, 10, 405-19.